PAST AND FUTURE

By

William H. McNeill

PHOENIX BOOKS

THE UNIVERSITY OF CHICAGO PRESS
CHICAGO AND LONDON

This book is also available in a clothbound edition from
THE UNIVERSITY OF CHICAGO PRESS

THE UNIVERSITY OF CHICAGO PRESS, CHICAGO & LONDON
The University of Toronto Press, Toronto 5, Canada

PREFACE 1964

THIS BOOK was written during the Korean War. It was partly a tract for the times and partly a preliminary sketch of *The Rise of the West*, for it did not then seem at all certain that public events would allow me time to complete the larger enterprise.

Apocalyptic fears have so far proved ungrounded, and the climate of opinion with respect to international relations is distinctly more relaxed now than it was twelve years ago. As a result, both the American and the Russian transnational alliances, which seemed so pregnant for the future in 1952, have become raveled and frayed instead of growing stronger. The reasons are familiar enough. As soon as ICBM's, armed with hydrogen warheads, had been emplaced and made ready for takeoff in a mere matter of minutes, their possessors' power was not only enormously enhanced but marvelously blunted as well. For now that both the Russians and we ourselves are seriously afraid of incurring instant destruction in the event of war, we and they are unable to muster much plausibility behind threats aimed against any of the less powerful states and peoples who may choose to defy our wishes or theirs, whether covertly as allies or openly as enemies.

A simulacrum of plural sovereignties has therefore come

to life again, far more vigorously than I thought possible in 1952. Perhaps this new constellation of international politics may prove as enduring as any other of times past. Yet surely unusual fragility is built into a regime that permits the weak to defy the strong because the strong are afraid of their own strength. Sovereignty on sufferance is not the same as sovereignty based on authentic local superiority over any and all comers. After all, the two really great powers of the world may always decide to co-operate with one another, at least long enough to allow each a chance to deflate the play-acting and posturing of contumacious allies and rebellious satellites. A definite division of the world into spheres of influence would be the prerequisite of any such arrangement. But this is a standard maneuver of international politics whose recurrence is far from impossible.

Indeed, if we and the Russians fail to make such a deal in the fairly near future, the prevailing balance of terror between us will undergo a drastic disturbance as other states acquire the capacity to manufacture the hydrogen warheads we and they now monopolize. It remains to be seen whether the world's peace can survive the complexities of a world divided among an indefinite number of sovereign states each possessing the capability of destroying all or a large part of the human population of the earth. Moreover, even if awareness of the risks of nuclear war maintains a precariously balanced system of separate state sovereignties indefinitely into the future, we must expect the restless inventiveness of our age to produce still other technical marvels that will disturb the balance of power in other ways.

Perhaps, therefore, in 1964 we are passing through a lull rather than inaugurating a prolonged peace. Catastrophe may come so suddenly as to take almost everyone by surprise. Tensions may mount again to something like the pitch of 1952. Or international relations may stumble along more or less as today, with the United Nations and other agencies of international co-operation maintaining or even consolidating their authority. We simply cannot know, and should be glad of our ignorance. Due reflection upon how little of the present posture of the world's affairs could be accurately foreseen in 1952 should both reinforce intellectual humility and whet naïve curiosity about the new surprises the future will continue to bring forth. Anything else would be abdication of our human condition.

The truly remarkable changes of the past twelve years do not perceptibly affect my understanding of the deeper past. Indeed, in rereading chapter ii of this book, I am struck by how little I learned from the years of reading that went into *The Rise of the West*. This is both reassuring and depressing. It suggests soundness of preconception, for the bare bones set forth in this essay, even when fleshed out with considerably more detail, proved capable of bearing their burden and did so with a modicum of grace. Yet the very success of such an enterprise implies intellectual ossification. Discrepancies and deficiencies in these preliminary formulations were disregarded—indeed not observed at all! Inability to recognize fundamental alternatives is, perhaps, a normal sign of intellectual maturity. It may in fact be prerequisite for intellectual creativity, since creativity requires a selective sensitivity to the entire range of potential data and stimuli.

On the other hand, these reflections may amount to no more than whistling in the dark to keep my courage up. In any case, it remains a fact that if I were writing the chapter on the past over again today, I would wish to alter a few turns of phrase, but nothing fundamental.

The next chapter, "The Present," stands up quite well also. Antagonisms between free and Communist states, between industrial and agrarian societies, and among the principal racial and cultural stems of mankind still constitute the main fracture lines of the contemporary world, and moral uncertainty has lost none of its actual and potential significance. To be sure, the ideological confrontation between communism and liberal democracy appears to be somewhat less prominent now than it was, and the conflict between cultural and racial groups is more in the forefront of the news than before. But such variations constitute rather a shift of accent than a change of shape.

Matters are far different with the chapter dealing with the future, for my remarks about the toughness of civil society even in the face of atomic war were premised on a conception of future war which seems now thoroughly archaic. If scientists are to be believed—and I do not doubt their truthfulness—human life might now be destroyed entirely as a result of a few days' (or even hours') exchange of missiles. Under these circumstances, the notion of a long war, lasting several years and requiring the mobilization of an entire society, loses plausibility. The whole thrust of the argument of the first part of chapter iv, based as it was upon the assumption that future struggles would conform in a general way to the patterns set in our time by World Wars I and II, now seems misdirected. In the event of a future world war, decision—or ultimate catastrophe—seems likely to occur very much sooner than it did in the great wars of the first half of our century. There will probably be no time to bring into action armed forces and matériel not already in being and emplaced before hostilities start. War may thus become more professionalized than in the recent past, when mass armies trained and equipped in large part only after the commencement of hostilities, constituted the decisive factor.

Increasing professionalization of war constitutes a partial return to conditions characteristic of early modern times, when diffused exercise of violence, characteristic of medieval society, was supplanted by standing professional armies, which quickly became so expensive that only great princes and kings could maintain them. Yet limited war, the corollary of early modern military professionalization, seems most unlikely to emerge from the wonderland of contemporary weaponry. Instead, whole cities, provinces, and peoples run the risk of instantaneous destruction at the hands of professionals ensconced in their dug-outs half a world away!

The enormously heightened risks of such a style of warfare obviously diminish its likelihood. No sane man will deliberately destroy self, country, and humanity entire. Blundering escalation of some conflict might still take place without any of the parties clearly willing total catastrophe; and madmen may ascend to positions of political command in the future as they have sometimes done in the past. Statistically speaking, in a world divided into a number of competing sovereignties, if we allow a long enough period of time for each and every nation to acquire a store of hydrogen warheads and of even deadlier weapons yet to be invented, one must count upon one or both of these circumstances arising. But in the short run, and on a time scale familiar to that of the individual human life, it remains comfortingly true that the risk of total war is sharply reduced today as against what it was a dozen years ago.

All this I entirely failed to foresee in writing chapter iv. Does it follow that the longer range anticipations of world government also have become worthless? Perhaps so, but perhaps not. Despite unforeseen episodes and radical changes in the operation of the balance of power such as those that the past twelve years have brought, it is still the case that the progress of science and technology continually facilitates the tasks of any future world administration. Communication and transport are becoming ever more rapid and capacious, while the arts of management and control—over men as well as over materials—steadily improve their precision.

Thus, for example, computers already exist that are capable of maintaining an indefinite number of bits of information about every living human being. Appropriate information fed into such a monstrous machine might in time create such an intimate and precise interaction among whole populations and individual persons as to reduce (or raise) us all to the level of the separate cells of some loosely organized creature like the Portuguese man-of-war, whose constituent parts are controlled and co-ordinated by chemical and electrical interrelations among the clustered cells that constitute the whole. We seem, in short, to be galloping toward the creation of the Leviathan of which political philosophers once dreamed—a Leviathan in which each man will have his place and proper function, calculated and assigned to him on the basis of most careful and precise statistical studies, sustained by data-storage and retrieval systems whose refinements we can only begin to imagine today. The technical means for such an evolution of humanity certainly appear to stand within our grasp, just as surely as do the means of total self-destruction.

The probability of the emergence of world government must be assumed to increase with its technical feasibility. The variety of circumstances through which such a regime might arise—whether by sudden coup or by gradual, almost imperceptible evolution—are as great as the variety of circumstances that might precipitate the hydrogen holocaust we dread. Perhaps therefore, despite the defects of foresight that now appear in chapter iv, it is still worthwhile to follow this exercise of the imagination, in order to think more about what any effective future world administration would require.

WILLIAM H. McNEILL

April 28, 1964

TABLE OF CONTENTS

CHAPTER ONE

THE PURPOSE OF THIS BOOK

THE PURPOSE of this book is to challenge its readers into a re-examination of their views of the past and future of humanity. It begins with a schematic analysis of world history and deals hastily with the social and political problems which presently beset mankind by way of preface to an account of what seems to me to be a likely course of future events during the next two or three hundred years. It concludes with some observations on what can and should be done by Americans in the immediate situation which confronts the world.

Obviously the attempt is audacious, perhaps foolhardy. The infinite variety of human affairs makes any schematic interpretation of past and present a travesty of the real complexity, and there is no need to emphasize the uncertainty of the future in an age when nearly all men feel that uncertainty pressing close upon their private lives.

History, indeed, is full of surprises and accidents, some of them trivial in their consequences, others of profound importance. And any honest student of human affairs must admit that the interaction of individuals, groups, communities, and peoples, of ideas and ideals, of institutions and traditions, of geography and technology, of simple hopes and panic fears—human life, in short, is so complex as to dizzy the understanding. It follows that certainty about either the past or the future is out of the question.

Yet, if we are to try to think about what has happened and will happen to large numbers of men over long periods of time, it is necessary to resort to generalizations and formulas in lieu of the infinitely detailed facts, many of which we cannot know. But it is important to take generalizations for no more than what they are: efforts to imprison in a mesh of words the real variety and individuality of men.

If we approach the interpretation of past and future in this spirit, generalizations and formulas may perhaps mislead us still, but we can hope for a saving flexibility of mind and of action.

Few men have the leisure or the stimulus to make any extended effort to understand what is happening around them. Yet it does not seem idle even for a tiny handful of men within a larger society to try to understand and to act upon their understanding of human affairs After all, human wills and ideas contribute to produce actual events. While it is true that a society cannot be transformed by any mere act of will, it is also true that the exact shape of future events is not predetermined by forces external to men's minds. Decisions and actions, sometimes made by individuals, sometimes by small groups, and sometimes by much larger aggregations of men, vitally affect what does happen; and the cumulative effect of a series of such decisions and actions may, over a period of time, transform the limiting social and physical conditions inherited from a given past and open new paths for human development.

Habit and emotion no doubt predominate usually when men must take decision; but there are times of crisis when familiar habits, customs, and institutions fail to provide adequate guidance. In such moments of history, ideas and programs of action evolved by men who happened to have the time and found the stimulus to think in longer, more reflective terms about human affairs have a chance to come into their own. When a partial breakdown of established ways upsets the whole life of a nation or of a group of nations, new ideas may rather abruptly win the assent of large numbers of men and move almost overnight from the realm of academic speculation into the world of practical action.

In recent American history the first phase of the New Deal was such a time. New ideas, new practices, and new men proved able profoundly to affect the established pattern of American life and institutions. Similarly, the Bolshevik and Nazi revolutions showed how a much more drastic redirection of Russian and German society could be brought about by ideas and programs of action which originated among a handful of individuals. It is because more crises surely lie ahead for all the major nations of the world, and because groups advocating the false, violent, and inhumane ideas and practices of a Hitler or of a Stalin are already everywhere in the field, that at least a handful of the men who hold dear the nobler traditions of Western civilization[1] ought to think hard and long about past and future and seek to find for themselves and for their peoples

1. No man who has been nurtured in the civilization of the West can hope to speak for the other civilized traditions of the earth, and it would be foolish to make the attempt.

a course of action and a long-range ideal which may serve as a liberating guide in time of future crisis.

In a rational consideration of past, present, and future it seems proper to try to separate an analysis of past trends and their probable future development from a direct statement of personal hopes and wishes. A man may ask first: How is the world likely to change if the impetus we have inherited from the past works itself out to a logical conclusion? Then he may turn to the question: What can be done and what should be done by the human groups to which I belong in order to bend the outcome in the direction of my wishes? And, having made such an estimate, our intellectual explorer may speak, act, and live in a fashion calculated to have the fullest possible effect upon the actions and attitudes of his own immediate circle, upon the affairs of his own nation, and, however slightly, upon the development of the world itself. Only so, it seems to me, can a man hope to achieve his full stature as a political animal; and only if a people contains within itself a body of such men may it hope to rise successfully to meet the challenges to familiar habits and institutions which future crises seem sure to present.

The hope of stimulating others to think in long terms about the past and future of mankind, rather than any partial accuracy of my particular analysis and forecast, is, then, the purpose of this book.

CHAPTER TWO

THE PAST

1

Human history may be viewed as a product of an unceasing conflict between two opposing psychological penchants. On the one hand, men are capable of insight into things, can imagine new combinations and arrangements, can conceive new ideas and create new mechanical or social devices—all through the operation of their intelligence. On the other hand, men are prone to habit, custom, routine, which, once established by repetition, tends to attract powerful emotional attachment simply because it is familiar, safe, and dependable. Each human life is dominated by habit most of the time, and so is every human society. Only so can we thread a path through the potentially almost infinite number of possible lines of action which confront us at each moment of every day. Habit and custom restrict our field of choice, leaving all but a handful of alternative lines of action on one side, beyond the scope of conscious attention. Without such a limitation of our mental vision we would probably be unable to make up our minds at all, and the elaborate integration of individual action with that of other men to make a functioning society would most certainly become impossible.

In simple stable societies, custom and habit provide a

standard response to practically every circumstance which may confront an individual from birth to death. Life under such conditions offers great psychological security, and it takes a very unusual personality or some unprecedented happening to introduce any but the tiniest, most gradual changes in the established way of doing things. Social change is therefore slow and occurs, if at all, almost unperceived by the members of the community. Instead, the tried and trusted ways of the ancestors are passed down from generation to generation and maintain unquestioned prestige together with compelling psychological force.

For nearly all of human history societies such as these prevailed everywhere: societies whose analogues exist today only in a few remote corners of the world to which civilization has not penetrated. I believe that the human make-up fundamentally fits such a stable, customary pattern of existence and that the shifting welter of uncertainty which pervades so much of contemporary life puts a severe strain upon all who are subjected to it. The emotional and habitual bases of our lives are still the same, or very nearly the same, as those of primitive men; but the society in which we live has been radically transformed. From this stems a deep malaise which in our own time encourages a widespread pessimism about progress and the future of mankind

But such pessimism is not well founded. Men are not entirely bound by emotion and habit; what most distinguishes us from other animals is the scope and power of human intelligence which can and does introduce change and progress into social life.

In the earliest ages of historical development there seems

reason to believe that periods of comparatively sudden transformation alternated with long periods of social stability. During the stable periods men were able, largely unwittingly, to consolidate custom and institutions after adapting them to a new pattern of social and technical relationships. Thus the series of inventions and changes which transformed hunters and berry-pickers into Neolithic agriculturists apparently occurred within a few hundred years, somewhere in the region of the Middle East; and the new form of society which resulted became for perhaps three thousand years a fairly stable adjustment to the newly discovered agricultural way of life.

From the first center in the Middle East, Neolithic village communities spread slowly but very widely over Europe and Asia and Africa wherever land could be found which was suitable for cultivation with the primitive implements then known. The next great revolution in the form of human society began in the flood basins of a few great rivers: the Tigris-Euphrates, Nile, Indus, and (much later) the Hwang Ho. In these river valleys successful agriculture demanded large-scale irrigation works to regulate the floods and bring fertility to the land. Once again, the establishment of the Sumerian civilization of the Tigris-Euphrates and of the Egyptian civilization of the Nile appears to have come rather suddenly; and, after priest-dominated cities had been established, a remarkable stability set in which survived with only marginal changes for a period of nearly fifteen hundred years.

We must imagine that Neolithic village communities seldom had contact with outsiders. Travel was limited by the length of a man's legs and very likely by superstitious fears of anything beyond the familiar horizon. What contact there was with forest hunters and other strangers was probably reduced to customary patterns which minimized the intimacy and extent of interchange. Trade in certain valuable objects such as amber and special stones did sometimes extend over long distances; but such a phenomenon was not incompatible with a generally isolated existence for each separate village community or group of communities.

Even the larger, more complex societies of the early river-valley civilizations must have lived in a very considerable isolation. Within the river valley itself, ships and rafts permitted relatively easy transport, at least downstream; but over the hills and far away was a different matter, for there men's legs and backs remained for long centuries the only regular mode of transport. Except for certain minerals and timber, there was little to tempt the valley dwellers away from their homes; and the relatively small communities that were able to maintain themselves on land not fertilized by the river floodwaters could not, at first, hope to attack the populous cities of the plain with success.

2

The subsequent history of civilized mankind can be considered largely as a product of the progressive breakdown of this isolation. The reason is this. When habit and custom, formalized into institutions, written into law, and supported by religious beliefs, are not exposed to the challenge offered by alien ideas, techniques, and manners, no very important changes in the sacred ancestral ways are likely to occur. As long as the old and familiar patterns of behavior continue to work smoothly, the overwhelming inertia of normal men's minds maintains things pretty much on a level. But, when contact with aliens becomes extensive, something has to be done. Sometimes it is possible to reject the new as unholy; but even such rejection is likely to lead to so strenuous a reaffirmation of the ancestral ways as in fact to change and transform them. The history of the ancient Jews illustrated this phenomenon; so strenuously did they reject alien religions that the Hebrew God of battles transformed his character and became the Yahweh of the prophets and priests.

Sometimes, however, alien ways recommend themselves and are willingly adopted because they seem to offer practical or aesthetic advantages. This takes place most conspicuously when a more elaborate civilization comes into touch with simpler, more backward peoples. The conquest of Rome by Greek art and manners provides an example of how such a change can occur by the willing choice of the recipient; and the reaction of the Japanese to some aspects of Western civilization illustrates a similar process in our own day.

Most often in history, however, what makes most powerfully for social change is the application of force. Alien ways can always be brought urgently to the attention of a people when the bearers of those ways are militarily powerful and threaten raids or conquest. In such cases, once again, the reaction may be one of rejection; but effective rejection often requires reorganization and military innovation at home. An example of this relationship is provided by the Persian wars which the Greek cities were able to win only as a result of the development of a formidable fleet, a fleet which in turn became the basis for the imperial career of Athens, with all the profound repercussions Athens' action had upon the history of ancient Greece as a whole. A second example might be the German reaction to the Napoleonic conquest. The Germans (or rather the Prussians) were forced to adopt some of the Napoleonic innovations in social and especially in military organization and, having done so, laid much of the basis for the rise of imperial Germany, with consequences from which the world is still trying to recover.

Equally, a military threat from outside may lead to conquest and mingling of alien and old ways within a new society. It is perhaps straining words to call such a situation a voluntary assimilation of the new; yet the effect is analogous, for a new social entity, comprising conquered and conquerors, emerges upon the scene of world history, an entity which may develop a common sense of social solidarity over a period of time. The histories of all the great empires of the world illustrate this pattern of cultural blending as an aftermath and by-product of a violent collision between alien peoples.

Whatever the outcome of contact between the bearers of mutually alien habits, institutions, and ways of thought, the result is always social change of greater or less magnitude and importance. The process is seldom a simple and direct borrowing; civilization is too closely meshed a web for any simple mechanical incorporation of some new element to be possible. Rather, when changes occur, adjustment throughout wide ranges of social life become necessary, and in the process of adjustment there is opportunity for recombination of differing ideas or practices into something quite new. In short, invention in the widest sense is provoked by such cultural immixture. There is, moreover, a tendency for the new invention and readjustment of social behavior to achieve a superiority over all the original ingredients—a superiority which may be practical or aesthetic.

Perhaps examples will make this generalized analysis more intelligible. Take the origin of Greek philosophy, for instance. It arose first in Ionia, where Greek conquerors came into intimate contact with autochthonous peoples of Asia Minor. This brought two very different religious systems into collision; the sky-gods of the Greeks and the earth deities of the Anatolians had nothing in common, and the myths associated with the two pantheons were equally alien to each other. Thus reflective men in the cities of Ionia were presented with incompatible explanations of natural and other phenomena, and there was no organized and authoritative priesthood to reconcile the differences. This was the situation that provoked men like Thales to try to explain things for themselves; and, since Thales was no more than an ordinary man, others after him felt no compulsion to accept his explanation as authoritative and definitive. They too could try to understand and explain. Consequently, the early philosophers boldly made the effort, each bringing a larger range of phenomena into the scope of his explanation or attempting to do so. Empedocles had a theory that embraced not only physical nature but the behavior of living things as well; and with Plato not only the physical and biological but social and political and epistemological questions came within the scope of rational examination and explanation. The result of these efforts was an understanding of the world aesthetically superior to anything that had gone before—far eclipsing in scope, breadth, and impressiveness the religious myths whose conflict had originally impelled men to embark upon the enterprise.

As an example of the development of a practical superiority from the blending of disparate social elements one might consider the origin of the Roman system of federal military organization. In ancient Italy, Italian tribal federations came into hostile contact with newly founded Etruscan and Greek city-states between the tenth and sixth centuries B.C. At first the Greeks and Etrucans were militarily (and of course culturally) superior to the Italians and drove them back into the hills of central Italy. Rome apparently was established as a city-state by Etruscan rulers; but, when in due course the Roman nobles revolted and overthrew their Etruscan kings, a new mixture of Italic and alien elements took form. The Romans combined the old pattern of loose religious association among tribal units with the new city-state form of social organization, modified both, and in time created a politico-military federation among simulacra of Greek and Etruscan city-states. A new and far more powerful political and military unit under Roman leadership thus emerged in the Italian peninsula. It enjoyed a marked practical superiority over each of the old-fashioned separate city-states; and Rome's new superiority permitted the conquest first of Italy, then of the entire Mediterranean world.

In more recent times the political organization which emerged from the Norman conquest of England provides a similar example of blending of institutions to produce a newly formidable unit. The Norman and Plantagenet kingdom of England was certainly superior as a practical organization of power both to the French feudal principalities, on the one hand, and to the Anglo-Saxon kingdom, on the other, whose institutions had been combined to create it. And one may view the contemporary rise of Russia as the consequence of a blend between czarist autocracy and Western technology: a combination which has raised the might of the Soviet Union far above that of any single nation-state of Europe.

The argument does not imply that every collision between peoples with alien ways of life leads to a superior blending and recombination of elements. Such is of course not the case. Failures and abortions are probably far more usual than successful recombinations, though, almost by definition, the failures bulk far less large in our historical records. But I do suggest that contact with alien ideas and manners provided the mainspring for historical development through most of the recorded past. Without such contact, whether peaceable or violent, men would not have been stimulated to change their ancestral patterns of life; the rate of social evolution would certainly have been vastly slower and would presumably have taken totally different paths.

If this be so, it should be possible to interpret the history of the world in terms of the successive manners in which men of alien cultures came into contact with one another. A history of particular instances of such contact would require volumes and far more knowledge than I can command; but for the purposes of this book we may simply distinguish four great epochs, marked off from one another by changes in the predominant mode of transport and communication through which alien societies came into contact with one another.

The first of these has already been touched upon: in the beginning men walked on their own two feet.

A second great epoch was introduced with the domestication of the horse. This gave men a new mobility and range in all those regions of Eurasia where grass grew naturally and could provide pasture for horses. This epoch started about 2000 B.C., and, despite the gradual rise of shipping as a supplementary channel of contact between alien societies, one may conceive the "equestrian" epoch of Eurasian history as lasting until about the end of the fifteenth century A.D.

The third epoch was introduced when ships came to link the great centers of civilization into an interacting whole. Although sea-borne commerce between India and the Middle East started several centuries B.C., and although Arab traders later ventured across the Indian Ocean and into the Pacific to reach the China coast as early as the eighth century A.D., these contacts remained only marginal. But when Europeans launched themselves upon the oceans of the world following the great explorations of the late fifteenth and early sixteenth centuries, a new and dominating partner speedily transformed the scale and social importance of the ocean commerce of the world. Europeans first revolutionized themselves and then the world and by their enterprise quite altered the scale and nature of contact between the great established civilizations not only of Eurasia but of the New World as well. It seems therefore proper to date the third great epoch from the time of the European discoveries, despite the injustice such a scheme may do to Arab (and to Chinese) sailors of the centuries just preceding.

Finally, a fourth epoch has just burst upon us: the age of mechanical transport over land and sea and through the air.

Throughout each of these epochs haphazard collision and contact between differing societies brought sporadic improvement in practical or aesthetic power, now to one, now to another, region of the globe. *Each epoch, however, was distinguished by an appropriate general pattern of political and cultural relationships*—a pattern which accorded with the methods and geographical channels of contact between alien peoples and civilizations which then prevailed. Whenever one epoch succeeded another, vast and world-wide revolutions in political and cultural relations followed within the span of a few generations until a new, though often precarious, equilibrium was established.

Let me try to make these generalizations more meaningful by describing what I conceive to be the leading characteristics of each of these four world epochs.

3

The Pedestrian Epoch.—This we have already touched upon. It was an age of isolated communities, each living for long centuries without exposure to any serious challenge from alien societies. Perhaps the more significant challenges to human ingenuity came from geographical circumstance; indeed, the Neolithic development of agriculture and the taming of the river floods in Mesopotamia and Egypt have been connected by some scholars with a gradual desiccation of grassy hunting lands which once stretched where the Sahara and Arabian deserts now extend.

The Middle East area was apparently the center in which both Neolithic agriculture and the river-valley form of civilized society originated. This gave the Middle East a head start, so to speak, over all the other portions of the globe. From the Middle Eastern center, agricultural techniques spread gradually through Eurasia and Africa. How this occurred must be a matter for speculation. Perhaps over long generations repeated migrations by small groups, driven to seek new land by the exhaustion of their old fields, steadily infringed upon territory formerly occupied, if at all, only by hunters. In other cases it seems possible that hunting peoples already on the ground borrowed agricultural techniques from neighbors.

The areas of contact between agriculturalists and hunters constituted perhaps the most significant social frontier during the "pedestrian" epoch. Along that frontier the strong and persistent challenge offered by the peasant way of life met the older hunting pattern of existence. The peasant was usually victorious. Like a great glacier, moving outward slowly from the Middle Eastern center, the peasant mass made its way through Eurasia wherever geographical conditions would permit.[1]

1. The expansion of agriculture continued long after what I have called the "pedestrian" epoch came to an end. Only very restricted parts of Europe, for example, had known the hoe and the sickle before 2000 B.C. The agricultural conquest of the main northern European plain came only after the Christian Era; and, indeed, the expansion of agriculture (though, in most parts of the world, no longer of Neolithic agriculture) continues to our own day.

The first few centuries after the peoples of Egypt and Sumer succeeded in establishing the more elaborate societies of the early river-valley civilizations saw no very significant change in the world balance which had been struck when Neolithic agriculture first began to spread. The very fact that the two civilizations exhibited a very close and remarkably successful adjustment to the special geographical conditions of the flood plains of the Nile and of the Tigris-Euphrates meant that transplantation to fresh ground was particularly difficult. Until methods of fertilization, fallowing, and crop rotation had been hit upon, permanent agriculture could scarcely arise where the soil was not watered and fertilized by river floods. (Neolithic farmers tilled a piece of land until its fertility was reduced, then started a new field where suitable ground could be found.) Hence radical changes were needed before the civilization of the river valleys could spread beyond the flood plains. In particular, the practical basis of royal-priestly power—the control of the flood and of the irrigation system, partly by engineering and partly by magic—could not be transferred to unirrigated land; and the rise of large political units was correspondingly retarded.

During the pedestrian epoch, then, the general world picture was one of a cultural "storm center" in the Middle East, from which influence radiated slowly to other parts of Eurasia and Africa.[2] Contact between alien communities

2. In the Americas the pedestrian epoch lasted until the advent of Europeans; and in the course of the thirty-five hundred years which intervened between the close of the pedestrian epoch in Eurasia and the European discovery of America civilizations based upon a quite different type of agriculture arose in Central America and Peru.

Incidentally, the introduction of the horse into North America by

was limited by the weakness of human legs; by the routine of agriculture, which required regular work in the fields; and by the absence of any strong attraction to adventure beyond the circle of territory exploited by the village community. Warfare was not unknown, but its prominence and social importance were far less than in subsequent ages. Indeed, archeological remains from European and Middle Eastern Neolithic villages seem to show a remarkably pacific society, disciplined not by war but by the seasons, and devoted to labor in the fields and to the pursuit of fertility for crops, beasts, and men.

It seems probable that under Neolithic conditions an ordinary family did not produce more than enough food to feed its own members in most seasons, soils, and climates. Professional warriors could thus find no means of subsistence; everyone, or very nearly everyone, had to work at the business of finding food. In the river valleys, of course, a substantial agricultural surplus was produced; but (at least in the Middle East) it was at first not warriors but priests who availed themselves of their religious powers to appropriate the surplus in these favored regions for the support of themselves and of elaborate temple establishments. Warfare between neighboring temple–city–states in both Mesopotamia and Egypt led in due course to the

---

Europeans worked a revolution in the life of the Indians quite comparable to the revolution which had occurred about three and a half millenniums earlier in Eurasia. The military power of the tribes native to the great plains of western North America was enormously enhanced by the acquisition of horses; and, had white men not intervened with crushing superiority, one can imagine something like a re-enactment of Eurasian history. At least it seems probable that the plains Indians would have been able to raid and conquer their neighbors, both southward and eastward.

establishment of kingdoms or empires. These states united most or all of the river valley under the authority of a single ruler or college of priests and even spread their power into neighboring territory.

Until the taming of the wild horse brought a new mobility and striking-power to the peoples who lived outside the irrigated river valleys, the dense populations of the flood plains had little to fear from their neighbors, who were far fewer in number, no more mobile, and no better equipped or disciplined for battle than were the people of the plains themselves. It followed that the military challenges presented by alien peoples from outside the river valleys were seldom serious; and, since their neighbors' wealth and cultural achievements were far inferior to their own, the societies of ancient Egypt and Sumer, like islands of civilization protruding from a Neolithic sea, found little fructifying stimulus from contact with their immediate neighbors. In the absence of such stimulus, both civilizations soon settled down to relatively fixed forms of expression, doing so rather rapidly after the revolutionary success of the first efforts to tame the swamps of the river valleys. By comparison with later epochs, the sustained pace of social change was snail-like.

4

The Equestrian Epoch.—The world balance which I have tried to sketch above was radically transformed when, about 2000 B.C., nomads and herdsmen of central Asia discovered the possibility of taming the wild horse and were able to harness his strength and fleetness to their own purposes. Horses were at first used to pull light two-wheeled chariots; later men mounted directly on their backs to acquire still greater speed and mobility over rougher ground. The geographical home of the horse nomads was the steppelands of central Asia and southern Russia, with a secondary center in Arabia and North Africa. Across the central sea of grass mounted men could move without difficulty for thousands of miles. The grasslands were ringed on three sides by the agricultural communities which had sprung up during the pedestrian epoch and abutted closely upon the river-valley civilizations of the Middle East.

This geographical constellation was not new in itself. The pastures of Asia and Arabia has supported wandering herdsmen for many generations before the horse was added to the ranks of the domesticated animals. What was new was the military balance which now came to prevail between the agricultural and the nomadic peoples. Peasant populations, unaccustomed to the horse, found a chariot or cavalry charge truly terrifying, as passages in the Old Testament bear witness; and the mobility of horsemen meant that mounted nomads could strike over long distances, arriving unheralded to catch the agriculturalists unprepared. The military advantages thus enjoyed by mounted men may be compared to the advantages of tanks over unsupported infantry in modern war; and the horse nomads were not slow to make use of their new-found strength. Beginning about 2000 B.C. they repeatedly overran, wave after wave, the river-valley civilizations of the Middle East, bringing violence and rapine with them and everywhere testing or breaking the established social and political organization.

Whenever such nomadic conquest took place, the newcomers established themselves as a military aristocracy. But, after a few generations, the conquerors regularly adopted most of the culture of their subjects, modifying mainly the political and military organization of the conquered society. It was only where the nomads overran less developed peoples—most notably in Europe—that they retained their own cultural traditions with only marginal admixture from below.

Rarely did nomadic conquest permanently destroy or even seriously interfere with agricultural life. The conquerors came not to destroy but to enjoy. Destruction of course often occurred, and sometimes on a great scale; but this was usually temporary and soon repaired by the patient work of peasant serfs, encouraged or driven to it by their new masters. From the point of view of the conquerors, the food and services which their new agricultural subjects could supply were too valuable to lose. Even the indigenous priesthood usually survived nomadic irruption, for, without the priests' magic power and astronomic calculation of the seasons, who could guarantee the harvest? And, without the professional administrative services of the priests (who enjoyed a monopoly of literacy and kept the written tax records), who could assure the collection of tribute and the discipline of the conquered peasant mass?[3]

3. A late example was the survival of the Greek Orthodox clergy in the Ottoman Empire. Compare, too, the place of the Chinese mandarins in the Manchu Empire. Early examples may be found from Egyptian history during the years of Hyksos rule; and the survival of priestly colleges in Mesopotamia under repeated waves of conquest is indicated by the retention of the Sumerian language for religious use long after it had been supplanted by the speech of Semitic conquerors in all other walks of life.

Despite the frequently superficial character of nomad conquest, the flights and upheavals, wars and raids, inseparably connected with such conquest repeatedly unsettled established societies and helped to maintain a state of flux in habits and institutions. Earlier ages had been, by comparison, undisturbed and stable.

Such conditions advanced the geographical spread of civilization. Consider, for instance, the importance of those distinguished refugees, the Philistines and the Etruscans, for the development of the primitive Hebrew and Italian peoples.

Disturbed conditions also tended to force improvement in the political, military, and technological organization of the agricultural peoples, for their conquerors naturally wished to retain what they had won, and only a strong military organization could prevent successful renewal of nomad invasion. The long succession of oriental empires, from the time of Hammurabi (*ca.* 1950 B.C.) and the Hyksos (*ca.* 1680–1580 B.C.) to the time of the Ottoman (A.D. 1354–1922), czarist (1480–1917), and Manchu (1644–1911) empires, often exploited but also served to guard their peasant subjects against fresh nomad encroachment. Each in its day had its measure of success. Whenever the wealth and numbers of the agricultural peoples were used to organize systematic military resistance to the nomads. it was seldom that their fewness did not tell against the raiders from the steppes. Tribes of horse nomads could not usually unite among themselves. When they did, they were capable of bursting with exposive effect upon the agricultural world, as was dramatically demonstrated by the Arab conquests of the seventh century A.D. and again by the greatest of all the historic waves of nomadic conquest, that led by Genghis Khan and his successors in the thirteenth century A.D.

It is worth emphasizing that the dominion of the horse nomads was limited by the shortage of pasture for their horses in the parts of Eurasia that had been taken over by agriculturalists. Whenever they went beyond the steppes to conquer alien sedentary populations, the nomads were compelled to modify and in the end to abandon their way of life. Large herds of horses and other animals were necessary to the nomads, but such herds could not be maintained without abundant grass. The necessary grassland simply did not exist in the semiarid regions of the Middle East and Mediterranean coastlands or in the naturally forested parts of western Europe, India, and China. Hence a more or less definitely fixed geographic boundary was set between nomandry and agriculture, and it was across this border that the central process of stimulus and counter-stimulus to social development took place for the better part of two millenniums. Even after a trickle of sea-borne commerce brought the great centers of Eurasian civilization into a new and fruitful contact with one another, the horse nomads, with their military prowess, remained an important element in the world balance until about the end of the seventeenth century A.D.[4]

4. Until the very end of the seventeenth century the Turks, the last of the nomadic imperial conquerors to come westward, were a serious menace to European nations; and the Manchus conquered China near the middle of the same century.

It was not until the time of Ivan the Terrible of Russia (1533–84) that Russian peasants began to expand on a large scale into the steppeland of the Ukraine and Volga region, thus starting the process of seizing per-

I would argue, then, that the horse nomads had their main historical importance in the military sphere, forcing the agricultural peoples of Eurasia to embark upon an almost unremitting effort to strengthen themselves against attack or rewarding failure to do so by making them accept new conquest from the steppes. But the nomads had a second important role: when they could not conquer, they traded, and as merchants they connected the great civilized centers with one another in a new and significant way.[5] At least as early as the time of the Roman (31 B.C.–A.D. 410) and the Han (202 B.C.–A.D. 220) empires, regular overland routes between China and the eastern Mediterranean had been established, over which toiling pack trains carried goods all the way across the continent; and with the goods came ideas and stimulus to new departures. It is possible to trace, for example, the influence of Greek art styles upon Chinese sculpture and of Indian religion upon Chinese religion; while, from the other direction, the introduction of silk making into the Mediterranean in the sixth

---

manently from the nomads their historic homeland. From the east, it was not until the 1930's that Chinese peasants were able to penetrate Manchuria in large numbers, displacing the Manchus from their ancestral grasslands.

Scattered agricultural communities had existed on the steppes earlier than this, and some had flourished for centuries. Yet they remained at the mercy of nomadic attack and sometimes were nearly destroyed by nomad conquerors.

5. In the strict sense of the word, nomads seldom if ever were merchants. But the itinerant merchant's way of life, traveling from market to market with his pack train of goods, bore a strong resemblance to the true nomad's life, spent traveling with his animals from pasture to pasture. Hence the transition from a nomadic pastoral to a nomadic commercial mode of life was easy and occurred repeatedly in the case both of individuals and occasionally of whole tribes.

century A.D. is a definite and datable example of the transmission of Chinese techniques to Europe. In these and countless other—mostly untraceable—instances, the great civilizations of Eurasia cross-fertilized one another through the mediation of the nomads and their cousins, the pack-train merchants.

Thus, with the taming of the horse (supplemented a few centuries later by the camel), the Eurasian continent became an interacting social whole, much more closely bound together than it had been or could be in the days when men had depended on their own legs and backs for transport. The horse nomads were like a fluid connecting the denser masses of agricultural settlement which had arisen on the borders of Eurasia—a fluid which percolated and penetrated into the agricultural areas whenever the local political organization or military prowess suffered decline; a fluid which unceasingly circulated over the inland sea of grass separating the main centers of civilization and, in so doing, acted as a conductor between them. New ideas, new inventions, new practices of many sorts could now spread from any point of origin within Eurasia to be taken up, modified, or rejected by peoples living thousands of miles away. There was usually no exact knowledge of whence new things had come; yet the human horizon had been vastly widened, and a continent-wide process of action and reaction had been initiated which kept social change alive as it could not have been kept alive had each civilization remained in security and comparative isolation, such as prevailed during the first centuries of river-valley life.

Yet one must beware of exaggeration. The horse nomads were primitive and brutal, and by no means did they consciously set out to stimulate or force the agricultural peoples along the path of civilization. Their conductive capacity was very limited; they were not philosophers or mathematicians and from the nature of their life could not themselves absorb or transmit such elements of civilization. Moreover, the military prowess of the horse nomads and the chronic disorder among them often interrupted trade routes and made it difficult and dangerous for civilized men to cross the grasslands in person. Hence it was a trickle, not a flood, that passed between such centers as Europe, India, and China. Until the seventeenth century A.D. each of these civilizations had essentially independent careers, fertilized and stimulated by one another and by the incessant millitary challenge provided by the horse nomads but never overwhelmed or shattered by alien influence or attack.

Thus classical-Western, Chinese, and Indian civilizations each developed a peculiar character and had a distinct and more or less self-contained history. This was not really true of the world bridge—the Middle East—where the center of nomadry lay close at hand and where cross-currents from China, India, and the West played more immediately upon the indigenous populations. The peoples of the Middle East were never allowed to live in peace for long and so could not develop along lines dictated by any inner momentum. Instead they were constantly jarred, twisted, and transformed by intervention from without. Living at a crossroads is often uncomfortable and dangerous, but it is also stimulating; and that was the position of the peoples of the Middle East as long as the highways of the world crossed the grasslands of Eurasia.

5

The world balance created by the interplay between nomadry and agricultural civilization has long since vanished. It permitted independent civilizations at the extremes of Eurasia; it gave the Middle East a special role as the pre-eminent middle man of the world; it left the Americas, Australia, and most of Africa out of the circle of interacting civilization; and it relegated Europe to a definitely subordinate position.

Yet it was from Europe that the next great forward leap was to come. It was Europeans who developed a civilization capable of using ocean-going ships to link the whole civilized world with new ties—ties that were much closer, stronger, and pervasive than anything raiding nomads and animal pack trains could maintain. Because of Europe's critical importance in the third of our world epochs—the epoch of ocean shipping—the development of European society during the preceding equestrian epoch deserves special attention. We may well ask: What were the peculiarities of European society that made it the seat of a civilization which was to break like a flood upon all the rest of the globe in the sixteenth and subsequent centuries?

First, one may distinguish a difference in the origin and subsequent character of European civilized society. When the horse nomads first burst into Europe, about 2000 B.C., they found only small, weak, and comparatively backward Neolithic village communities to victimize. There was little in the culture of these peoples that seemed to the nomads to be worthy of imitation. As a result, it was the language, religion, and even, with important modifications, the way of life of the nomads (in this case, Indo-Europeans) that came to be established in the various countries of Europe. In some parts, notably Greece, a more developed society confronted the conquerors, and it was there that a distinctively European civilization first arose from the intermingling of the nomadic and the pelagic ways of life; but even ancient Greece was predominantly Indo-European in speech, religion, and social institutions.

This fact had important consequences. In such parts as the Middle East, China, or India nomadic invaders regularly settled down to exploit the indigenous peasantry, becoming landlords and aristocrats, officials and warriors. In Europe no such life of ease and glory was possible. There was no numerous and passive population to exploit. Warlike herdsmen, when they had left the vast grasslands behind them, were compelled to rely increasingly upon agriculture; but, in doing so, they did not entirely abandon herding, nor did they shed their warlike habits or attitudes. Even when a growing land shortage pushed herding into marginal land and made agriculture the unquestioned center of European economic life—even after this long process of modification in the ancestral nomad ways had been completed—farmers still remained warriors too. Indeed, embattled farmers—the Greek hoplite and the Roman legionary—were able to resist and modify the aristocratic structure of society which first emerged from Indo-European conquest; and, while the military balance between mounted aristocrat and peasant foot soldier shifted back and forth from time to time through subsequent European history, it never happened that the ordinary peasants of Europe were for long entirely divorced from the possession and use of arms. A much more warlike and tough-fibered society resulted from this fact than any that could exist where armed conquerors trod upon the submissive necks of an exploited peasantry—as was the normal pattern in the civilized parts of the world.

The extraordinary bellicosity of Europeans is something which men nurtured in the traditions of Western civilization seldom fully appreciate. We are far too much the children of our ancestors to realize how extraordinary their attitude toward war really was. Traditionally, Indian and Chinese peasants have been unwarlike in a sense and to a degree seldom if ever equaled by Europeans.

The difference is apparent in the great world religions. One element in Christianity derived directly from the God of Battles worshiped by Hebrew nomads; and Christian writers regularly and naturally resorted to military analogies, viewing the terrestrial world, indeed, as one long, uninterrupted field of battle between sin and salvation. So far as I know, neither Buddhism, Confucianism, nor Hinduism accord any comparable prominence to military similes and images; only Islam betrays its nomadic inspiration by frequent resort to the language of war. In general, the imprint of nomadic peoples was deeper in the Middle East (and northwestern India), where Islam made its principal conquests, than it was in India or China. Yet, in comparison with Europeans, the peasants of most Moslem countries, too, have traditionally been a nonmilitary population, unable to challenge the long succession of military rulers who have exploited them and unwilling to fight wholeheartedly under their rulers' direction against usurpers at home or fresh challengers from outside.

Taking world history as a whole, one sees that agricultural peoples characteristically are not men of war. Only in marginal districts, especially in mountain fastnesses, where the soil could not easily be made to yield sufficient food to sustain the inhabitants, have peasants taken to the sword in any number. Since about 2000 B.C. in most of Eurasia, peasants have seldom been more than passive sufferers from the warlike activity of their rulers, nearly all of whom sprung directly or indirectly from the horse nomads.[6]

Yet European peasants have often turned their plowshares into swords and have regularly admired and striven to emulate (or to defeat) the man of battles instead of merely fearing and hating him as their analogues in other civilized societies have normally done. It seems plausible to connect this difference with the manner in which European society came to birth: Indo-Europeans dismounted from their war chariots and harnessed their oxen to the plow but never forgot or entirely abandoned the bellicose habits of their nomadic ancestors.[7]

6. This is not altogether surprising. After all, the work of the fields can take nearly all a man's time, while the nomad's life is one of comparative idleness, since flocks and herds attend to their own increase. A nomad's main occupation must be the defense of his animals and of their pasture grounds, and of course the best defense is to attack and raid neighboring peoples' flocks and herds. War is thus a normal pursuit for the nomad; it is not for the peasant.

7. I do not mean to imply that the Indo-Europeans altogether exterminated the agricultural peoples whom they found already on the ground in Europe. But I do suggest that the ethos of the invading tribesmen rather than that of the Neolithic agriculturalists predominated in the blend which presumably occurred.

The warlikeness of Europeans has taken many forms through history and has often worked great intestinal damage upon Europe, not least in the most recent war. Yet there is another aspect to war as practiced in Europe which helps to explain why European technology so markedly outstripped that of other centers of civilization: from the beginning of European history to the present day, warfare has repeatedly forwarded technical change and improvement. Its action has been both negative and positive. On the one hand, war breaks into established routines of life and compels men to give up old ways for new. On the other hand, the desire for security against attack or for victory in attack has stimulated men to devote their ingenuity to the development of new and more efficacious ways of killing one another.

Many examples of the impact of war upon technology could be advanced from European history. Consider the mechanical investigations of such a forerunner of modern science as Leonardo da Vinci. He was employed as a military engineer by the duke of Milan, and many of his inventions and speculations upon things mechanical were inspired directly by his interest in finding better ways of fighting. In a peaceable society Leonardo would not have been employed as a military engineer and might well have confined his energies to the decorative arts. The recent development of jet airplanes and of atomic research are but the latest examples of how military aims may advance technological mastery over the forces of nature.

Aside from turning men's minds to deliberate technical innovation, warfare may also forward technology by presenting new demands for various products already being made on a relatively small scale. The whole history of the metallurgical industries of Europe could be written in terms of demands created or expanded by warring sovereigns, states, and peoples. Metals were generally too expensive for all but a very few peacetime uses until war demand had created new, larger-scale, and more efficient methods of mining, refining, and working the ore. This was as true of aluminum in the twentieth century A.D. as it had been of iron in the twelfth century B.C.

War's negative function of breaking down established ways of life is equally, if not more, important for the advancement of technology. When old methods fail for whatever reason—and warfare nearly always interferes with things as usual—an effort to patch together an acceptable substitute mode of action becomes imperative. Usually the makeshift is unsatisfactory; but there are also occasions when the new path proves inherently superior to what had been familiar before. An example of such war-born improvement in our own day might be the development of managed economies. During World War I, and more pronouncedly during World War II, new devices of economic administration were created by all the warring powers which promise to banish in the future the periodic depressions which were such a prominent characteristic of former economic life.

Some may feel that the concomitant drawbacks of a managed economy are so great as to make the gain dubious. Perhaps a less controversial instance of war-born technical advance may therefore be in order. Consider how it was that the potato came to be established as a staple of European diet. Under the climatic conditions of northern

Europe, the potato can in most soils produce far more calories per acre than can grain; yet this obvious advantage was not enough to persuade Europeans to accept the new crop when it was first introduced from America. On the contrary, it was only under the stress of war, when the normal routine of agriculture was upset, that European peasants turned to the potato and found it good.[8] It is, in fact, usually possible to equate increases in the use of potatoes with outbreaks of war, from the time when the Cromwellian conquest of Ireland drove the Irish peasants to adopt the new crop in the mid-seventeenth century to the marked increase in potato-growing that occurred in Europe during World War II. Yet, once driven by the hardships of war to accept the new crop, European populations had at their disposal a much extended food supply; and this was one of the factors which permitted the extraordinary growth of European population in the late eighteenth and early nineteenth centuries.[9]

8. The reason is not far to seek. In wartime, potatoes are a much less precarious crop than grain. Grain must be harvested within a rather short and sharply defined period of time; not so potatoes, which, if need be, can remain in the ground for weeks or months, where the very labor of digging will keep them relatively safe from ravaging soldiers.

From the military and marauding point of view, grain is far preferable to potatoes, for the latter are bulky and spoil easily in transit. Hence only if grain cannot be found will an army commissariat look for potatoes at all. Since European armies regularly and as a matter of course lived largely off the land they fought over, until after the Napoleonic Wars, it mattered a great deal to local peasant families whether, when the soldiers came by, they had reserved some ground for potatoes which they could fall back upon when their grain bins had been emptied by military foraging parties.

9. One of the revolutionary by-products of the Seven Years' War (1756–63) and of the Napoleonic Wars (1799–1815) was the establishment of potatoes as the principal food staple of the northern European plain, from

Similar examples of the impact of warfare on European technology could easily be multiplied. Taking it all in all, one can hardly believe that Europeans would have been able to develop their technology as in fact they did without the bellicosity which made their warfare not solely a matter of concern to a handful of ruling aristocrats but an affair involving nearly all ranks and occupations.

A second peculiarity of Europe which contributed to making European civilization so powerful as it in fact became by the seventeenth century was a matter of geography and climate. The European climate was far more forbidding than that of India, the Middle East, or southern China. It necessitated greater effort and activity than was required by the warmer, more inviting climes of other civilized centers. In early times this was certainly a disadvantage; but, when suitable clothing, suitable buildings, and suitable crops and farming methods had all been brought into use, Europe's cold and damp turned into an advantage. Because the minimum base level of physical

---

Belgium through Poland. The rise of Germany in the nineteenth century would scarcely have been possible without the new food resource provided by potato fields. Until about 1870 large-scale import of food into Europe from overseas did not occur. (Railways had first to span the great interior plains of the New World and of Australia before wheat for European markets could be grown on any large scale.) If Germany had been compelled to rely on cereal crops, great agglomerations of population in industrial cities could hardly have been fed; but the potato, by multiplying (in many cases as much as four times) the calories that could be produced per acre on German farm lands, made it possible to feed men clustered around the coal fields to work in new factories. This agricultural change provided one of the essential bases for the extraordinary growth of Germany's industrial and military power in the nineteenth century.

existence was higher in Europe than in warmer regions, men required more things to keep them vigorous, and to make those things men had to work harder than in softer climates.

Not only this: habits of activity were inculcated by the weather itself. For most of the year, to be up and doing was the only way to keep warm. No Indian holy man could long contemplate infinity while shivering in Europe's winter; and, when the medieval monks imported Middle Eastern asceticism into Europe, it underwent a characteristic adaptation to the climate. Not Simeon Stylites but Benedict of Nursia set the pattern of European monasticism, and his rule required holy activity and work as well as prayer and abstinence.

Only northern China, of the other centers of Eurasian civilization, could boast such a demanding climate; but northern China lacked an additional advantage which geography conferred upon Europe, namely, the great inlets—the Mediterranean, Black, and Baltic seas—which penetrated the European land mass both north and south. Of these, the Mediterranean was of course by far the most important for ancient history. It was tideless, and its coasts abounded in small harbors suitable for small ships; in addition, it enjoyed long summer months in which storms were rare. All this made seafaring relatively easy, even in primitive, ill-equipped ships; though the sailor's life had its share of terrors for the peoples who lived around the Mediterranean in ancient times, as Paul's journeyings remind us.

Nevertheless, the Mediterranean was in a very real sense the mother of classical civilization. Shipping became an essential basis for the economic life of the Greek and Greco-

Roman cities of the ancient world. Raw materials and a large proportion of the food required to maintain the town dwellers had to come from overseas. Only by using sea transport could the great cities of classical antiquity tap the food and raw-material resources of distant parts of the Mediterranean littoral; only so could they swell their population beyond the limits set by local food supply.

Until ships could traverse the ocean with reasonable confidence and regularity, the full advantage of Europe's geographical shape—a relatively narrow peninsula, threaded by navigable rivers and penetrated by bays, estuaries, and shallow seas—could not be felt. In Roman times ships did venture upon the tidal and stormy waters of the north and west, but on the whole the Romans preferred to depend on roads and never fully mastered the gray northern seas. Hence, in Roman times, sea-borne commerce never assumed the importance in northern Europe that it had in the south; and the development of cities and of the civilization of cities was correspondingly inhibited.

A second very important obstacle to the rise of civilization in northern Europe was the incomplete success with which the Romans and their subjects were able to adapt the agricultural techniques of the Mediterranean to the soils and climate of the north. The flat, low-lying plains of northern Europe were naturally covered with heavy forest alternating with swamp. Except on sandy, loess, or chalk soils, drainage was so poor that winter grain drowned and spring grain could not be planted until too late in the season to assure the harvest. Roman and pre-Roman agricultural settlements in northern Europe therefore tended to restrict themselves to hilltops and slopes and to specially pervious soils where natural drainage was unusually good.

The invention that first made the fertile plain lands of northern Europe suitable for agriculture was the moldboard plow, an instrument unknown to the Romans and unnecessary under Mediterranean climatic conditions. By the pattern of its operation the moldboard plow created an artificial system of drainage, shaping an otherwise flat field into shallow ridges and ditches. This served to draw off surplus water from the fields and permitted the survival of winter grain and a much earlier planting of spring crops. The moldboard plow came into general use in northern Europe between the fifth and ninth centuries A.D. It gave the inhabitants a much more dependable and abundant food supply than they had been able to find earlier. It meant also that an agricultural surplus could easily be produced—a surplus upon which warriors, merchants, and artisans could be maintained on a scale impossible before.

The establishment of a new and far more productive system of agriculture in the so-called "Dark Ages" was matched by the conquest of the seas. The Viking raiders were among the first to plow Europe's northern and western seas and feel fully at home upon them. For about two centuries, between about A.D. 750 and 950, they took over a role in European history almost exactly analogous to that assumed by the horse nomads of central Asia in world history at large. By taking advantage of the mobility of their ships, the Vikings were able to raid the settled agricultural communities of the south until, in due course, they were either absorbed as conquerors or repelled by newly organized defenses. When sea raiding ceased to be rewarding, the Vikings and their descendants in more southerly lands turned to sea-borne commerce; and other Europeans soon imitated and surpassed them.

When seamanship had advanced to a point where tides and storms of the ocean created only tolerable risks, northern Europe could successfully imitate the much earlier economic development of Mediterranean Europe; and, having a larger expanse of fertile soil, numerous and navigable rivers, richer fishing grounds, and larger mineral resources than the south, these regions were gradually able to overtake and surpass the economic development of the older Mediterranean centers.

Thus it happened that the role of shipping in medieval Europe came to be almost exactly comparable to its role within the Mediterranean in classical times. Medieval cities, like the classical cities before them, were supplied with raw material and food brought from afar by water. Overland transport was important when goods of high value in proportion to their bulk were in question; but ships carried the plebeian staples like raw wool, timber, fish, grain, and, by the fifteenth century, coal, upon which Europe's economy had come to depend.

It is worth emphasizing how profoundly the possibility of shipping bulky and cheap articles over long distances shaped the whole pattern of European economic development. In medieval and early modern times, European artisans did not characteristically excel in the production of fine ware for the delectation of a wealthy and cultivated ruling class as tended to be the case in China, India, and the Middle East. Instead, European skill tended to run to the production of plain, useful things like woolen cloth and ironware. Production and trade were not centered upon the task of supplying luxuries to an aristocracy or to an officialdom but instead served the wants of a much larger (and as time went on, an ever increasing) section of the entire population. The more imperative wants of the common man in a chill climate forwarded this development as compared with conditions in the Orient; the stronger and more effective assertion of their wants by a common people that never entirely abandoned the ethos of nomadic warrior-conquerors certainly explains something too. But without the cheap and easy transport provided by shipping, it could not have occurred.

The peculiar geographical and technical conditions within which European economy developed help to explain how it was that European artisans were, generally speaking, far inferior to Arab, Indian, or Chinese workmen in luxury crafts but were able to supply the wants of the general population on a scale and with an efficiency not equaled elsewhere. Conversely, the fact that oriental civilizations depended to a much larger extent upon overland animal transport tended to restrict their long-distance trade to articles of high value in proportion to their bulk; and this confirmed the emphasis upon luxury production which the social structure of China, India, and the Middle Eastern countries encouraged anyway.

This is by no means a wholly adequate explanation of the special bias shown by European economic development during the Middle Ages and in the early modern period. Political and religious influences were certainly at work, and doubtless other factors should also be accorded weight in any balanced effort to explain why it was that, in comparison with the other civilizations of Eurasia, Europeans had by the sixteenth century developed a more tightly integrated exchange economy, in which a larger section of the total population took active part, depending even for staples of daily life upon sea-borne commerce which extended its web over all the seas that surrounded and penetrated the heart of the European peninsula. One thing, however, seems clear. It was the special character of the European economy, together with the peculiar bellicosity of Europeans, that combined to make possible the extraordinary revolution in world relationships whereby, between the seventeenth and the nineteenth centuries, Europeans became able to stamp their imprint upon all the other peoples of the earth.

There was a third dimension of the European achievement during the equestrian epoch of world history which should not be passed over without notice. Europeans were deeply indebted to the ancient Greeks and to the long line of scholars and curious men who followed in the paths first explored by the Greek philosophers and scientists. The revolutionary possibilities of applied science were not imagined, much less experienced, until after Europeans had opened the oceans of the world to their shipping; yet long before then one of the pervasive characteristics of European thought was the confidence Europeans placed in the powers of human reason.[10]

The social barriers between European scholars, on the one hand, and artisans and soldiers, on the other, were very great, yet probably not so great as in other civilizations

10. This was true of the medieval Scholastic philosophers as well as of the men of the Renaissance or of the eighteenth century, even though the Scholastics recognized a realm of revealed and authoritative truth which later thinkers tended to neglect or to deny.

of Eurasia. Even before the seventeenth century, when technical and social progress became so rapid, it is perhaps right to attribute a part of the European technological achievement to the efforts of scholars and scientists to apply their powers of reasoning and observation to the understanding of the natural world. Alchemists and metallurgists had their points of contact at least as early as the thirteenth century, and so did geographers and mariners, mathematicians and merchants (the abacus, Arabic numerals).

The other great civilizations of Eurasia were by no means indifferent to rational thought. The Moslem peoples shared the inheritance from the ancient Greeks to the full, and it would be rash and presumptuous to assert that Europeans gave any larger range or greater value to reason and intellectual insight than did the Chinese, Indians, or Arabs. But one can say safely that, in combination with Europe's other circumstances and peculiar conditions, the rationalistic tradition inherited from the past and nurtured from generation to generation by monks, clerics, and scholars entered into a growingly fruitful contact with the practical everyday life of artisans, merchants, sailors, and soldiers and became one of the essential elements promoting European technical and military progress; and, further, that such cross-fertilization between theory and practice was less characteristic of the intellectual activity of the mandarin, brahmin, or mullah than of the European scholar.

These sociological, geographical, and intellectual peculiarities of Europe help to account for the fact that, by the beginning of the sixteenth century, Europeans had acquired a mastery of the arts of war and peace that gave them decisive advantage over all the other peoples of the world. Yet one must not fail to credit the stimulus Europeans constantly received from other civilizations. Such crucial inventions as the compass, paper, gunpowder, and printing all originated outside Europe, though enterprising Europeans put them to new uses which soon far surpassed their significance in the societies of their origin.

In point of fact, until about the fifteenth century, European technical skill and military power developed at a pace not much if any greater than that of the Middle Eastern peoples. Certainly the Ottoman Empire was a match and more than a match for European states on the battlefield as late as the time of Suleiman the Magnificent (A.D. 1520–66); and even in the sphere of navigation and shipping, in which Europeans came to excel by the time of the great discoveries, the Arabs of the Middle East were for centuries superior to the West. Arab merchants adventured by sea as far as China in the age of the Abbasside caliphate (A.D. 750–1100) at a time when Europeans were only beginning to master the ocean around them. Through the centuries a trickle of sea-borne trade and cultural contact between the Middle East, India, and China continued to grow slowly and came to supplement the older overland routes across central Asia and over the mountains of India's northwestern frontier.

Indeed, the advent of what I have termed the epoch of ocean shipping was gradual if one considers the entire Eurasian scene. It was sudden only from the European point of view. What is mainly surprising was not the fact that, at the end of the fifteenth century and the beginning of the sixteenth, Europeans joined the circle of Middle Eastern,

Indian, and Chinese sea commerce by rounding Africa. The development of the arts of navigation over centuries had fully prepared the way for this achievement. Rather the surprising thing was Europe's extraordinary reaction to the discoveries, Europe's bold and reckless exploitation of the new opportunities, and Europe's self-transformation and retransformation in response to the stimulus of the new contacts which flowed in so suddenly not only from Asia but from America as well. It was, in fact, the reaction of Europeans to their own achievement which ushered in a new epoch and transformed the balance of the world from the pattern gradually developed during what I have called the equestrian epoch, when, under the stimulus offered them by the horse nomads, independent but interrelated Eurasian civilizations took form and structure in each of the great agricultural areas of the continent.

6

The Epoch of Ocean Shipping.—The discoveries of Portuguese, Spanish, Dutch, and later of English and French explorers transformed the balance of the world in a manner analogous to the transformation worked by the taming of the wild horse. The ocean spaces became paths of commerce and contact between the peoples of the world; and, since ships could carry larger quantities of goods more safely and cheaply than pack trains could ever do, since they could carry soldiers, missionaries, and merchants as well as goods, since they could reach the coasts of all the habitable world and return as easily as they had come—for all these reasons, the intimacy and scale of contact between alien peoples and civilizations reached a new level of intensity almost at a single leap.

The revolutionary effect of the discoveries and of the trade and conquest that followed in their wake is hard to grasp. The effect upon Europeans, who within a single generation saw new worlds opening before their startled gaze, who saw new products come flooding in from the Americas and from Asia, who heard tales of wonders, wealth, and adventure undreamed by their ancestors, and who could feel that they were in some sense masters of all that opened before them can only stagger our jaded twentieth-century imaginations. A world in which new continents, exotic civilizations, idyllic savages were suddenly unveiled can only be likened to what we should think if interplanetary travel should lead to the discovery of new forms of life and civilization sufficiently like our own to seem comparable, yet sufficiently different to seem incredible.

The impact of European civilization upon other parts of the world varied from case to case and was sometimes long delayed, as in Japan. Yet everywhere it was profound and disturbing. Europeans could and did feel elated by their achievement; other peoples could only be offended, frightened, or bewildered by the newcomers with their unpredictable, rough, and greedy ways, their guns, their ships, their energy, their power. Nevertheless, in the anciently civilized parts of the earth, where long traditions, massive populations, and complex institutions supported the indigenous ways of life, the European onslaught did not overthrow or destroy existing society. Despite all difficulties, the civilizations of India, China, and the Middle East maintained a recognizable individuality and a more or less conscious and deliberate resistance to European ways.

There is a certain parallel between their reaction to Europeans and their reaction to the attacks and conquests they had so often suffered from the horse nomads of Asia. Wave after wave of nomads had overrun the Middle East, China, and India, and, after working some changes in the indigenous civilization, each successive wave had been absorbed or driven out. Europeans came by a new route: over the sea. But their advantages of mobility and military power were comparable to those so long enjoyed by the nomads. And, whether they conquered, as in India, or were driven off, as in Japan, Europeans, like the nomads before them, could not erase the age-old civilizations they challenged so fiercely.

But these parallels are misleading. Europeans were no longer simple barbarians, and their civilization was not such that Asian peoples could absorb its impact without profoundly changing their own ways. Thanks to their ships, Europeans usually were able to keep close contact with their homeland—a thing the nomads seldom could or perhaps seldom wished to do. Moreover, European civilization, stimulated by the new and dizzy adventure upon which it had so unexpectedly been launched, had a most disturbing way of transforming itself from generation to generation. The techniques Europeans disposed of and the methods by which they dealt with the peoples of Asia changed constantly; and, as European methods changed, European power and example continually undermined the ancestral institutions and relationships of Indian, Chinese, and Middle Eastern civilization. All this had no parallel in nomadic conquests, and in time it called forth unparalleled transformations in Asian civilization—transformations which in our own day are only beginning to take shape and definition.

The effect of the opening of the ocean routes upon Europe itself was at least as great as the effect upon the other civilizations of Eurasia. Transformations of the economic and political balance within Europe are well known; the eclipse of the Mediterranean areas and especially of Italy and the rise of the countries fronting on the Atlantic were hastened by the new discoveries. More important for our purposes was the fact that the whole pace of social change within Europe received a new and extraordinarily powerful impulse. The stimulus from other civilizations which Europeans had received slowly but steadily through the long centuries of the equestrian epoch was tremendously enlarged. Fresh discoveries, inventions, innovations of all kinds came upon Europe with a rush.

An important consequence of this experience was the discredit which new information cast upon parts of the intellectual tradition which Europeans had inherited from the ancients. Theophrastus, it soon became clear, had not described the plants and animals of the Americas; nor had Aristotle dealt correctly with geography and astronomy. Instead of revering the wisdom of the past, interpreting it to fit the contemporary scene by appropriate glosses and minor additions or emendations, Europeans were driven to reject the authority of many of the books they once had accepted, and, with varying degrees of reluctance, scholars came to admit that the moderns had surpassed the ancients in one field after another.

This was a fundamental revolution of mind and took at least two centuries to come to completion. Sweeping rejection of the intellectual authority of the past ran counter to one of the deepest of human tendencies: the tendency to accept the familiar and endow it with an unexamined and unchallenged validity. But, as European men of learning gradually convinced themselves that they had surpassed the Greeks and Romans, a sort of heady self-confidence arose in them—a confidence in their own powers of reason and observation which seemed both justified and confirmed by the extraordinary growth of natural science in the seventeenth and subsequent centuries. Scientific progress in its turn prepared the way for the deliberate and conscious linkage between science and technology which constitutes what is probably the most important contemporary spring of social change.

The idea that men could, by taking thought and by making observations and experiments, discover the secrets of nature and then invent machines and devices by which natural forces could be made to serve human wants and wishes only gradually demonstrated its truth and, in doing so, achieved its contemporary prestige. Even after men like Francis Bacon had formulated the ideal of systematically seeking to find new technological applications of science, the inertia and skepticism of practical men and the prejudices of men of learning did not at once disappear. It was, indeed, only in the late nineteenth century that great industrial corporations came to accept as normal the practice of maintaining experimental laboratories in which men were employed to make systematic efforts to improve products and industrial methods. Similarly, the universities of the Western world have scarcely more than a century behind them since research in natural science and its practical application came to be considered as a normal and important part of the function of a university. Yet, long before the nineteenth century, the cross-fertilization between natural science and technology had been developing in Europe, and developing at a steadily increasing rate.

The transformation of methods of textile manufacture which occurred in England in the eighteenth century—a transformation which has often been rather misleadingly called the industrial revolution—was largely the work of practical men who had no notable familiarity with the work of scientists. But this development was an episode in a much larger and profounder change—a change which could better be called *the* industrial revolution, namely, the conscious and systematic application of the insights of natural science to transform and retransform the processes of production and transport.

As that occurred, the world witnessed the birth of a new and immensely potent engine of social change. Reason applied to things won, and continues daily to win, amazing victories over the forces of inanimate nature; and human society all round the globe is staggering under the impact of new techniques, new products, and new ideas about the nature of the physical world—novelties which seem to emerge from laboratories and factories at an ever increasing tempo.

Rational insight, I have argued, has from the beginning of human history been the principal source of social innovation. For centuries and millenniums reason acted sporadically. It came like a spark struck off when established habits and customs, from whatever cause, failed to function as expected; and it was in the hurly-burly of contact between alien peoples that this sort of accidental rational reorganization and invention found its main scope for action. But in Europe, between the sixteenth and the nineteenth centuries the use of reason to transform things to suit men's wishes became deliberate, systematic, conscious. It was as though human society had suddenly found eyes. Technological progress ceased to resemble the path of a blind man seeking to make his way along some rough and dangerous track, beset with pitfalls and dark alleys. Instead European scientists and technicians moved ahead like young men rejoicing in their strength, and European society dragged along in their wake, stirred, excited, and at the same time racked and bewildered by what was happening.

Inanimate nature has not been the only sphere in which Europeans attempted to apply deliberate, rational control. During the French Revolution men such as Robespierre hoped to be able to use reason to transform political institutions, overturning an irrational and ineffective form of government inherited from the past in favor of a manmade machine, designed, the revolutionaries fondly hoped, to serve men's wishes and needs. Despite the fact that the French Revolution went down to military defeat, the central idea—that government was and should be a creature of human contrivance, designed to serve human wishes and convenience—won acceptance in most of western Europe in the course of the nineteenth century, and in the twentieth it has become almost a shibboleth all round the globe.

This political revolution is familiar in all history textbooks, where it figures as the rise of liberalism, nationalism, and democracy. A further and more recent extension of the solvent force of rational, instrumental thought to human affairs is seldom more than partially recognized. Yet during the first half of the twentieth century inherited social and economic institutions and customs have been deliberately altered in all the leading countries of the world, often very drastically, in order to make the social energies of men serve some appointed goal more effectively than was possible under the old established patterns of conduct. Bolshevik practice in Russia was the most conspicuous and extreme example of this change; but all the leading nations of the Western world have shared, at least sporadically, in the development of new administrative techniques for exercising social and economic control over great masses of men. War mobilization, both in 1914–18 and in 1939–45, was the main forcing house for this latest application of conscious manipulation to human affairs. During the two world wars millions of individuals submitted their daily activities to the control of government officials—a control which, I think, it is not fantastic to compare with the control engineers are accustomed to exercise over inanimate machines.

Indeed, the intellectual revolution of the seventeenth, eighteenth, nineteenth, and twentieth centuries, the industrial revolution of the eighteenth, nineteenth, and twentieth centuries, the political revolution of the nineteenth and twentieth centuries, and what might be called the social revolution of the twentieth century all bear a strong family resemblance. Each is a conscious attempt to use reason to transform inherited ideas and practices into something more agreeable; and each involves serious and difficult moral problems. Some of these problems I will attempt to describe below; here it is enough to mention that science has in our own time seemingly turned upon itself by discovering the profound irrationality of mankind, and to observe that political and social engineers or would-be engineers confront questions of ethical choice which can hardly be solved by any conceivable exercise of reason.

So far we have considered in very general terms the consequences of the inauguration of the epoch of oceanic shipping for the established civilizations of Eurasia. What of the rest of the world? Where Europeans found weak and underdeveloped societies on the ground, the effect of their arrival was generally quite different from the effect they had upon the civilized peoples of Asia. Primitive populations could not resist European encroachment; and in some very large and important areas of the earth a process was initiated which may be compared to what happened when the Indo-European horse nomads invaded Europe itself.

Just as the Indo-Europeans broke up the Neolithic village communities of northern and western Europe, substituting a form of society created largely from the elements of their own barbaric culture, modified to fit the geographical conditions of their new homeland, so their European descendants broke down and destroyed the native life of areas of the world such as North America, the southern part of South America, Australia, and the steppes of Eurasia. In each of these regions Europeans were able to build a new society constructed from the elements of their own civilization and peopled largely by men of European race.

There were transitional zones, areas where the native ways of life staggered and nearly collapsed under European assault but survived at least in the sense that the indigenous population was able to perpetuate itself biologically while adapting itself to the general framework of a society established by European invaders. Central America and the northern parts of South America were such areas. European destruction of the Aztec and Inca life was only partial; but the existing framework of society in Mexico and Peru is largely European in form, and men of European descent occupy a dominant position in the resultant mixed society. Something analogous may be developing today in South Africa and New Zealand, where after an initial and nearly fatal shock the original inhabitants of those countries seem to be successfully reasserting themselves within a generally European social framework.

It is an interesting coincidence, perhaps a significant one, that just as the nomadic irruption into the partial cultural vacuum of Europe at the beginning of the equestrian epoch created in the fulness of time the dominant world center in the epoch of ocean shipping, so the irruption of Europeans into the partial cultural vacuums of North America and of central and northern Asia during the epoch of ocean shipping has led to the establishment of the two great political states—the United States of America and the Union of Soviet Socialist Republics—which currently exhibit the most successful adaptation to the fourth of our epochs: the epoch of mechanical transport. Certainly these two states have begun to enter upon the heritage of political dominance over the world, which, during the epoch of ocean shipping, rested securely with Europe. Because of the peculiar significance of Russia and the United States in the contemporary world balance, their development during the epoch of ocean shipping deserves special attention.

7

When English and French explorers first visited the eastern coasts of North America, they found a rather primitive society on the ground, not much superior in technical equipment to the society which their Indo-European ancestors had once found in Europe more than two and a half millenniums earlier. It was therefore not difficult for European settlers to displace the native inhabitants; but it was impossible for them to exploit Indian labor, since the Indians refused to adapt themselves to the servitude Europeans sought to impose.

It is, perhaps, worth asking why Europeans were unable to exploit the labor of the Indians of North America while they succeeded in transforming the Indians of Mexico and Peru and Negroes brought from West Africa into a usable labor force. Differences between Spaniards and Englishmen in dealings with the natives of the New World hardly seem adequate to account for the facts, nor does any theory of some intrinsic difference of temperament or bodily toughness as between the Indians of the south and those of the more primitive north seem plausible.

Perhaps the key lies in the primitive character of the society which prevailed in North America when Europeans first came on the scene. One may suppose that when men live in a tightly knit community, following a customary round to which profound emotional attachment adheres, then any fracture of the community deprives its constituent

members of any desire or willingness to live under such
radically new conditions as those offered by a European
plantation. On the other hand, when a society has evolved
toward a degree of civilization, with the looser social ties
that larger societies imply, then individuals are more easily
pried loose from any particular mode of life and adapt
themselves more successfully to new conditions, no matter
how oppressive or disagreeable. At any rate, it is a fact that
both the Indians of central and northern South America
and the Negroes from West Africa came from societies
which had already reached a level of primitive civilization.[11]

Whatever the reason, in most of North America, European conquerors and settlers were compelled to work
the land and develop its resources themselves, applying the
methods of farming and the artisan skills they had brought
with them from their European homelands. In time, a
modified replica of European society was thus established;
but, as long as cheap and rapid overland transport did not
exist, the great landlocked expanses of the center of the
continent could only be occupied by relatively simple
farming communities. Where ships had access, along the
Atlantic coast and up the larger rivers, trade and manu-

11. The analogy of disease is perhaps instructive. It is well known that
isolated human communities run the risk of annihilation by pestilence if a
new infection is suddenly introduced, whereas communities in which a
given disease is endemic are relatively immune to epidemic. Perhaps social
change is like disease. A stable society runs the risk of total collapse if some
sudden blow from outside compels abrupt change, whereas a society which
has become inured to knocks from outside and which has inaugurated a
process of making compensatory changes within may immunize its members from total despair and psychological disintegration, even should the
society itself go under as a result of fresh assault from outside.

facture analogous to that of Europe could and did develop quite rapidly after the first settlement; but the backwoods required the railroad before a modern type of industrial and commercial society could be established away from the head of navigation.

Long before the advent of the railroads, however, European settlers in North America found it relatively easy to explore the vast expanse of the continent. Their military superiority to the native inhabitants was so great that none but geographical obstacles and the rivalries of the various European nations themselves checked the expansion of state power westward until in due course the Pacific Ocean was reached by the then independent United States of America. A vast political unit was thus established, matched, on the north, by the similarly vast Dominion of Canada, whose development lagged about two generations behind.

The modern history of the Russian state bears some resemblance to that of the two great states of North America. Beginning about the middle of the sixteenth century, Russian peasants started large-scale encroachment upon the grasslands of southern and southeastern Russia— lands which for centuries had been the preserve of horse nomads. What made their advance possible was the rise of Russian state power, which by the time of Ivan the Terrible (1533–84) was able to demonstrate a new-found superiority to the remnants of the Mongol state in the Volga region and by the time of Peter the Great (1689–1725) was able to compete on equal terms with the more vigorous Ottoman power to the south.

Once the obstacle of nomad military superiority had

been overcome, the Russians faced an expanse of grassland and wilderness comparable in extent to that of North America. And just as explorers and hunters traveled westward in North America as pathfinders for pioneer farmers, so, in Siberia, Russian explorers and hunters penetrated eastward to the Pacific, which they reached before the end of the seventeenth century. The migration of Russian peasants was much slower and indeed cannot be said to have yet been completed; but throughout the seventeenth, eighteenth, and nineteenth centuries a large but relatively inconspicuous movement took place. Thousands of families traveled southward into the Ukraine and to the regions of the Lower Volga, while other thousands migrated eastward into Siberia, setting up new farms and establishing a European (or para-European) form of society as they went.

The breaking of the steppelands of Asia to the plow continued throughout the nineteenth century and was far from complete at the time of the Bolshevik Revolution. Stalin forwarded the process by deliberate policy, for one of the by-products of the collectivization of agriculture in the Soviet Union in the 1930's was the breakup of the last stronghold of the age-old horse-nomad way of life in Kazakstan.

Just six years before the Bolsheviks took power, the overthrow of the Manchus in China (1911) opened the grasslands of Manchuria to Chinese settlers; and a strong current of migration soon began to flow from the crowded peasant lands of northern China into Manchuria's empty spaces—a current which by the 1930's had transformed these steppes, which the Manchu emperors had kept safe for their horses, into farm lands.

The agricultural tide from Europe and the agricultural tide from China met therefore at the Amur River in the mid-1930's; and, when they did so, one of the major actors on the stage of world history—the horse nomad of Asia—practically disappeared. With his disappearance the last trace of the equestrian epoch of world history faded into the past.

The geographical vastness of both the Russian and the North American states was a direct result of their position on the frontier of European civilization, where, from the seventeenth to the nineteenth centuries, European pioneers equipped with European guns and agricultural methods came into contact with more primitive peoples whose military prowess and way of life could not stand against those of the newcomers.

Before the development of cheap and rapid overland transport, the vastness of the Russian and American states could not be translated into a correspondingly great military or economic strength. Without easy transport, the landlocked plains could only support a nearly self-sufficient type of agricultural community, spread relatively thinly on the ground, and unable to tap much of the mineral and other resources of the earth underfoot. Hence until after the middle of the nineteenth century, when railroads first began to open up the interior of America and of Russia, the agricultural giants to the east and to the west of Europe remained relatively weak, relatively backward, relatively unorganized when compared with the commercial, industrial, and military strength of western

European nations. Save where navigable rivers brought the back country into the stream of ocean commerce (and in Siberia the fact that the rivers drained northward to the frozen Arctic Ocean deprived them of most of their value in this connection) the heartland of both North America and Siberia remained peripheral to the balance of world power.

These limits to the development of America and Russia in the pre-railway age were but two instances of the situation in which all the continental heartlands found themselves during the epoch of ocean shipping. European influence did not penetrate far from the head of navigation anywhere in the world; and when, as in Africa, navigable rivers scarcely existed, the penetration of the continent was not seriously undertaken until the latter part of the nineteenth century. Indeed, much of the interior of the "Dark Continent" was not even explored by Europeans until David Livingstone's (d. 1873) time.

The general world balance of the epoch was thus one which gave a peculiar importance to the littoral of every continent. The frontier between nomadry and agriculture no longer occupied the central, critical role in world history. Instead the coastline of every continent came to mark the point of contact between Europe and the rest of the world's civilizations. Western Europe, itself a peninsula which could be said to have no heartland out of the reach of ships, became the acknowledged leader of the world, and European states acquired political control over a very considerable fraction of it. The Middle East lost its age-old primacy as the land bridge of Eurasia and became, relatively, a backwater. The circle of interacting human societies was expanded to encompass the whole globe, thus collapsing the separate worlds of Eurasia, America, Australia, and Africa which had earlier existed in almost total isolation from one another. The axis of the world came to run not between nomad and farmer within the continent of Eurasia but instead between European seafarer and all the other peoples of the globe. Moreover, within each continent a definite social gradient was established between the backwoodsmen of the interior and the commercial-industrial populations of the coast lands. Dominance regularly rested with the dweller by the sea, especially with the European dweller by the sea.

The political and economic world balance to which we are all accustomed—or were until very recently—was created between the sixteenth and nineteenth centuries as an adjustment to this epoch of world history. The European colonial empires, the cultural, military, and industrial primacy of Europe, the passivity of Asian civilizations under the blows dealt them by the hands of Europeans, and the relative inactivity of the United States and of Asiatic Russia in world politics—all these familiar landmarks of nineteenth- and early-twentieth-century world affairs were directly related to the epoch of ocean shipping which we have been considering.

But, since about the middle of the nineteenth century, Europe's place in the world, and with it the entire structure of the world balance, has been shifting rapidly as a result of the inauguration of a new epoch—the epoch of mechanical transport. Both the suddenness with which the change has come and the radical nature of the adjustment of world relations which is and will be necessary to accommodate political and economic institutions to the epoch of mechanical transport are fully comparable to the revolutions precipitated in the twentieth century B.C. by the appearance of the conquering horse nomads and in the sixteenth century by the advent of ocean-going European ships.

8

The Epoch of Mechanical Transport.—The spread of railroads to the continents of the world after the middle of the nineteenth century opened up their interiors to large-scale industrial development for the first time. But invention did not stop with railroads. Almost simultaneously (measured by the time scale of universal history) men discovered how to build all-weather roads and how to make automobiles and trucks to travel over them; how to communicate instantaneously by telegraph, telephone, and radio; how to build steamships; how to fly through the air; and now, it seems, men may even be able to traverse space by means of rockets. This tremendous outburst of improvement in the means of transport and communication, begun scarcely more than a century ago, was of course the result of the application of natural science to technology. Most of the inventions originated in Europe. Being first introduced there and more rapidly developed in Europe than elsewhere, for a time the new modes of transport and communication supported and even intensified European supremacy over the rest of the earth.

But in the long run it was not Europe that benefited most strikingly from the new inventions. On the contrary, the general effect of the new means of transport was to bring the full weight of the continental land masses of the world into the economic, military, and political balance.

In China and India mechanical transport at first extended and widened European impact. New Delhi was a monument to the Indian railroad system, which supplemented and largely superseded the river and coastal transport that had earlier set the pattern of British power in India. And in China rivalry over rights to construct and operate railroads into the interior introduced a new era of more intense European economic and military intervention in that country.

But before very long the greater intimacy and wider extent of contact with Europeans which resulted from these changes in India and China acted powerfully to stimulate the Indian and Chinese populations to resist European influence. It may not be too much to say that the railroads and associated improvements in transport and communication have made, or seem well on the way to making, India and China into coherent nations, self-conscious and organized as no earlier Indian or Chinese state ever was or could be.

But the full consequences of the new epoch in Asia have not yet manifested themselves.

The same may be said even more emphatically of Africa, where the opening of the interior to European exploitation as a result of improvements in transport brought engineers and plantation managers into contact with relatively primitive peoples.

So far it has been the heartlands of North America

and Siberia that have profited most strikingly from the inauguration of the new epoch. With the railroad and other improvements in mechanical transport and communication, the vast states erected by the Americans and the Russians when they were still predominantly agrarian nations became the scene of rapid and successful industrialization; and, as industrialization proceeded, the power and wealth of the two nations increased until in our own day it has come to overshadow the separate nation-states of Europe. Europe has thus been deposed from world leadership by the daughter-societies to east and west.

The advantages which accrued to America and to Russia as a result of their industrialization were partly temporary. Exploitation of virgin natural resources and the fact that American and Russian engineers were able to avail themselves of European experience when they set out to build new mines and factories frequently brought startling results. One may expect these advantages to fade as American and Russian industry grows older; but the margin of advantage they confer in comparison to European industry is still very great and will undoubtedly remain so for a long time to come.

Counterbalancing these advantages was the lack of skill which men newly brought from the fields inevitably exhibited when first confronted with complex modern machinery. The centuries-old artisan traditions of Europe produced (and continue to produce) workmen who excelled American and especially Russian skill. But such skill is not an unmitigated blessing. It may act as a powerful brake upon the introduction of labor-saving, mass-producing machine monsters whose operation would threaten skilled workmen with technological unemployment. Indeed, one may compare the industrial position of contemporary Europe with the industrial position of the oriental civilizations at the time when European traders and adventurers first came into contact with them in the sixteenth and seventeenth centuries. Today the skill of European craftsmen can produce articles of luxury that command a world market, just as the silk of China and the calico of India did three centuries ago. But articles of mass consumption, such as Europeans once could produce better than any other people because their machinery, raw material, and transport were superior, can now no longer be turned out from European factories at a price that competes easily with the products of American factories. West European production of consumption goods is undoubtedly superior to that of Russian factories today; but this arises from the fact that the men who direct Russian industry have not chosen to concentrate their effort upon consumption goods. In the fields where they have concentrated, notably armaments, Russian mass production does excel that of European states in quantity and, at least sometimes, in quality as well. Whether Russian armaments are produced more cheaply cannot be said, since data for comparison are lacking.

The advantages of the United States and of the Soviet Union in an era of industrial technology are not all accidents of their late arrival as industrial powers. The very size of the political unit which the pioneer settlers and soldiers created has had the effect of giving industrial technology a freer scope than it can have in a Europe divided by political boundaries into small and mutually hostile states. Within Russia and America none but physical obstacles stand in the way of combining resources drawn from hundreds or even thousands of miles apart. Great mills and factories can draw their sustenance from nearly half a continent, restricted only by the physical difficulties of transportation. Similarly, the size of the internal market within each country encourages the establishment of vast enterprises devoted to the mass production of goods on a scale that European factories cannot easily match.

These two advantages over European industry are permanent so long as Europe remains politically and economically divided. One may say that full development of modern industry requires a political unit as large as (in truth larger than) the United States or the Soviet Union. Only so can industrial managers have assured access to the raw materials and component elements they need for the industrial process; only so can the mass market which large-scale industry requires be protected from political obstruction; only so can the mobility of labor over long distances and among vast populations be easily attained.

It is worth emphasizing the advantages which the mere size of the political unit brings under the conditions of modern industrial technology. Pittsburgh could not have become what it is if the iron ore of Michigan and the coal of Pennsylvania had been divided from each other by a political frontier such as divides the iron ore of Lorraine from the coal of the Ruhr. Nor could Magnitogorsk have been created had the coal of the Kuznetsk and of the Don been politically cut off from the iron ore of the Urals. Detroit could not have become the center of such a gigantic automobile industry were it not possible to sell cars all over the United States without let or hindrance from local political authorities; nor could the tractor works of Stalingrad have been built on such a grandiose scale if the Soviet government had not required tractors to till the entire expanse of the Soviet Union.

Similarly, the rapid development of new centers of industry both in the United States and in Russia during the second World War could hardly have occurred if a vast population owing a common political allegiance had not existed thousands of miles away from the new sites upon which factories were erected—a population among whom individuals could be found, willing or unwilling, but still available, to build and then to man the new assembly lines.

The political boundaries of Europe, and the social, linguistic, and historical divisions which these boundaries represent, stand as almost insuperable obstacles to any comparable flexibility and efficiency of industrial production. Only when the Germans succeeded briefly in beating down the political obstacles to the free play of industrial technology during the second World War (and that not completely) did Europe acquire something comparable to the industrial advantages which come, as it were automatically, from the mere size of the American and Russian political units. Germany's defeat in the war was also Europe's defeat in the sense that a bid for world power based upon a European political unit failed. Soon after Hitler's defeat, Europe came to be divided into two mutually hostile parts; and each part now finds itself at least partially dependent on a power located outside the traditional center of European civilization. It would be hard to imagine a more dramatic symbol of the dethronement of Europe from the political and economic leadership of the world—a leadership which seemed so securely hers in the epoch of ocean shipping.

But while the decay of European world power is already far advanced, and while the world balance based upon that power has already been overthrown, the pattern of the future has only begun to emerge, and at best its features can be only dimly seen. This is not really surprising. In the long view of human development, which we have here tried to take, the world epoch in which we live and gasp for breath is still very young, hardly more than one hundred and fifty years old. The inheritance from the days of ocean-centered transport is still writ onto the world political map; and it is only rational to expect adjustment, probably violent adjustment, to be necessary before new institutions and relationships can be found that will be capable of restoring something like a balance to the world.

CHAPTER THREE

THE PRESENT

1

THE ABOVE ANALYSIS of the
past suggests that humanity is now confronted not only
by a need to adjust itself to another shift in the pattern of
contact between alien societies. Adjustments of that sort
have proved both drastic and difficult in former ages, and
the advent of mechanical transport and communication
would presumably in itself suffice to precipitate fundamental changes in the balance of the world. But, in actual fact,
the new modes of contact between alien peoples can
properly be regarded as an expression of an even more
fundamental change. After all, modern devices of transport
and communication are instances of what I have called the
industrial revolution (i.e., the systematic application of reason to the improvement of economic processes); and the
industrial revolution (when so defined) is in its turn but a
part of a general shift in human outlook and practice whereby men have tried to serve some appointed end more
efficaciously by transforming themselves, their fellows, and
their physical environment in conformity to rational
calculation.

The consequence of this revolutionary attitude and practice has been an unprecedentedly rapid rate of social change,
arising no longer mainly as a haphazard by-product of col-

lisions between alien ways of life but instead springing from the minds of men who deliberately and systematically seek out new methods, new techniques, and new ideas.

But, although human intelligence has been used as never before to fire the boilers of social change, mankind has not miraculously shed its tangled inheritance of habit and impulse, of tradition and feeling, of custom and instinct. Human irrationality is as real and as powerful as ever. We face our contemporary difficulties with a psychological nature little if at all different from that with which men have faced the world since the beginning of history.

What seems to have happened to Western civilization in the last two or three centuries is a drastic separation within the body social of the two opposed and yet complementary psychological penchants—the impulse to innovate and the urge to stand fast—which at the beginning of this book I suggested might be taken as the starting point for our survey of the past. A handful of professional innovators has established itself within the bosom of Western society. Their discoveries, inventions, ideas, hopes, and motives are in no appreciable degree derived from or paralleled in the thought and feelings of the general mass of the population. Instead we have an isolated professionalism; yet paradoxically, despite all the technical abstruseness of their specialism, the professional innovators' innovations keep world society on the boil—everywhere in motion, everywhere in flux, everywhere uncertain, unstable, and uncomfortable.

To be sure, one is always tempted to exaggerate the significance of one's own age. It flatters our self-importance to feel that we participate in peculiarly crucial transactions of world history. Yet if I am right in emphasizing the importance of the development of deliberate, systematic application of reason to find better ways to accomplish some purpose, then it seems correct to argue that the crisis confronting our own age is in fact greater than that any earlier generation of mankind has faced. Power, over nature and over men, has increased, and the velocity of social change has likewise increased; the result is that, in a given length of time, far greater social transformations can, and indeed must, occur. Consequently, human affairs have never, I think, been pregnant with such a wide variety of possibility as they are now. This is true because so many institutions and habits in so many lands have been undermined and shaken by untoward, unexpected, and unaccountable experiences. Indeed, a variety of possibilities implies prior confusion; and the actualization of some of those possibilities implies prior destruction.

This patently seems to be our present case. A casual reading of newspapers conveys some sense of the confusion which everywhere reigns. Wars and rumors of wars have provoked vast preparations for war in the most powerful nations of the world, while poverty so deep as to verge on famine stands as a constant threat to nearly half the population of the earth. International conflicts are matched by conflicts within many nations; and the cumulative insecurity generated by these and other conflicts destroys the peace of mind of millions.

The confusion around us may be regarded as reflecting three principal cleavages, which combine in varying proportions to exacerbate each particular problem. These are: (1) the political cleavage between Communist and non-

Communist states, especially the rivalry between the United States and Russia; (2) the economic cleavage between industrialized and nonindustrialized nations; and (3) the racial and cultural cleavage between Western and non-Western peoples. There is also a profound moral uncertainty which affects not only the men of the West but all the peoples of the earth—an uncertainty which makes every phase of social conflict more painful and more acute. Let us consider each of these in turn.

2

The Political Cleavage.—World War II and its aftermath rather abruptly changed the scale and pattern of world politics. The nation-states of Europe which began the war did not survive to end it. Instead, victory and defeat came to transnational organizations of military and economic power. The Germans subdued and then organized most of Europe into a single unit; and it was the resources and manpower of continental Europe as a whole which permitted them to fight so long and so effectively against the foes they had raised against them. The Japanese had less favorable ground for their attempt at empire-building, since most of the areas they conquered in the first months of 1942 were relatively undeveloped and could not add much more than raw materials to the warmaking power of the Japanese Empire. Yet in the Far East, too, the Japanese co-prosperity sphere transcended merely national scale, uniting the coastal and island areas of the Far East and the southwestern Pacific into a single whole.

Among the victors the same thing happened. America

and Britain exerted varying degrees of economic and political control over North and South America, Australia, most of Africa, and a segment of Asia. From all this vast area they were able to draw resources, from parts of it they drew manpower; and by a variety of financial and administrative expedients Anglo-American officials were able to organize most of the world to wage war against their enemies.

Russia entered marginally into the Grand Alliance; but the major effort of the Russian government was confined to the tremendous expanse of the Soviet Union itself. Nevertheless, the size as well as the variety of peoples which inhabit the Soviet Union make it misleading to consider the U.S.S.R. as comparable to the traditional nation-states of Europe. Stalin's achievement in the war showed that his government had succeeded in organizing Soviet resources and manpower into a warmaking unit comparable to the supranational units created during the course of the war itself by the Japanese, the Germans, and the Anglo-Americans.

The main impulse which drove the Germans, Japanese, Anglo-Americans, and Russians to create these vast organizations of power was the desire to increase their respective military strengths. The panoply of modern war has become exceedingly complex. Only an enormous industrial plant can create and maintain it. This in turn requires access to widely scattered raw materials and an elaborate administrative apparatus to control and co-ordinate the entire process of production, distribution, and consumption of military goods. But no complex industrial society is completely self-sufficient; and even if one were, in time of war it would still be foolish to neglect any opportunity of using resources or labor available in other lands, thereby adding to one's own strength while simultaneously denying an advantage to the enemy. War as it has come to be fought in our time therefore impels its protagonists to expand their power over whatever regions of the earth lie within reach. To an unprecedented degree, contemporary military technology rewards bigness: not only bigness of battalions, but bigness of industry, bigness of population, and bigness of space. Indeed, only very big states can any longer wage independent war.[1]

These facts suggest that the days of the sovereign nation-state on the European scale are numbered. Yet no automatic obliteration of traditional political units is to be expected. It is worth noting that during the last war the great powers did not seriously consider annexation of all the lands over which their practical power came to extend. Except in the Far East, where Japan's conquests came largely at the expense of European colonial empires, old established units of government were usually allowed to stand more or less unchanged, with legal claims to sovereignty unimpaired. But, in reality, such sovereignty was dissolved in greater or less degree by the actions of the great power within whose sphere the particular small nation-state hap-

1. Before the age of mechanical transport an invading army had to live off the land to a very considerable degree; and this necessity put a sharp limit upon the practicable size of any force designed to operate over long distances and for lengthy periods of time. Given appropriate discipline and equipment, a relatively small political unit could therefore meet any invading force on more or less even terms. How different the situation is today, when armies numbering millions can be supplied from bases thousands of miles from the actual field of battle!

pened to fall. "Friendly" governments were maintained or imposed; a variety of administrative officials were dispatched by the great power to supervise the mobilization of whatever resources it required and could persuade or force from the other nation; financial, transport, and trade regulations fixed by the great power stimulated or forced compliance with its wishes; and propaganda and information services attempted to convince the satellite peoples that co-operation with the dominant power was both morally right and practically prudent. By devices such as these, national barriers were broken through with varying degrees of thoroughness in different parts of the world.

Instead of a world divided between sixty-odd independent and equal governments, as prevailing legal theory presupposed, the war years presented the spectacle of four and only four genuinely independent centers of power, around which were grouped clusters of client states and dependent areas. In Europe, to be sure, countries like Sweden, Portugal, and Spain existed as buffers and transition zones without falling clearly into any one of the four great-power areas; and the outer reaches of the Anglo-American zone retained a wide degree of independence, verging toward open opposition in the case of Argentina. But these exceptions existed not so much because of the independent strength of the neutrals but rather because none of the four great warring powers judged it worth the military or moral cost to bring the recalcitrants to heel.

This wartime pattern of power was conceived by Americans to be a transitory thing, like the emergency controls imposed upon the domestic economy of the United States itself. Moreover, the United States fought the war on behalf of national self-determination and democratic self-government—high principles which could, at least partly, be translated into the will to prevent the establishment of new and formidable military empires in Europe and the Far East. The perpetuation of an American or of an Anglo-American domination over most of the earth on the lines which had been laid out during the war thus seemed out of the question in the years 1945–47. American principles, American habits of thought and feeling, and the passionate desires of the other peoples of the earth all forbade such a step.

The result was a relatively speedy dissolution of the special machinery of economic and military administration by means of which the war had been conducted. The American government tried to withdraw from its extraordinary wartime activities in other countries. Soldiers came home, and the future security of the world was left largely to the United Nations. The Foreign Economic Administration was abolished, and the future economic stabilization of the world was intrusted to private channels of trade and investment, supplemented by special organs of the United Nations.

Or, rather, such was the hope and intention of the American government and people in 1945 and 1946. But withdrawal and dismantlement of the wartime machinery was never complete. Troops remained in Germany and Japan, and new American naval and air bases remained in commission both in the Atlantic and in the Pacific areas. Moreover, economic crises, mainly in Europe, called for extraordinary loans, which, especially after 1947 when the Marshall Plan was proposed, brought officials of the United

States government into more and more intimate contact with what would once have been considered the internal affairs of other countries. In particular, American officials acquired considerable influence over the economic and military policies of western European and some Far Eastern nations.

Beginning in 1947 the policy of the American government came to be directed toward the creation of something very like the wartime pattern of transnational organization. The North Atlantic Treaty Organization, with its various subordinate military and economic authorities, was the principal fruit of this effort. In the Far East nothing as conspicuous as NATO came into existence, yet the United States established, maintained, or expanded special economic, military, and political relations with such parts of the world as Japan, South Korea, the Philippines, Formosa, Okinawa—relations which taken together extended American influence all the way across the North Pacific in a fashion not so very different from that in which NATO extended American influence across the North Atlantic.

Beginning in 1947, indeed, the American government and most of the American people who took any notice of such questions at all had come to think of themselves as leaders of a "free world," as against the "Communist world" dominated by the Russians. The two worlds waged what aptly came to be called the "cold war." In proportion as the cold war fell short of total war, so the organization of the free world fell short of the integration achieved (for example) within the Anglo-American sphere of influence during World War II. But, despite the fact that many features of transnational power organization which had been developed in wartime were absent or only embryonic in the free world during the years 1947–53, the parallels were nonetheless unmistakable. In spite of much reluctance and in the face of all traditional obstacles at home and abroad to such radical innovation, the United States, as leader of the non-Communist world, re-created the main outlines of the globe-encircling organization of power with which the Anglo-Americans fought the second World War.

The major motive which impelled the United States to return so extensively to wartime patterns was, of course, fear of Russian and Communist power. Immediately after the war, the Russians established a group of client states along their western frontier, thus bringing to an end the precarious independence which eastern European states had enjoyed between the first and second World Wars. Economic and military motives presumably guided Stalin. He wanted the resources of eastern Europe to help repair the war damage to the Soviet Union; he also wanted to set up a security zone along his western frontier. Stalin may have hoped to win such military preponderance in Europe as to make any future attack from the west impossible. But what seemed security to Stalin seemed aggression and cynical disregard of wartime promises to the nations of western Europe and to the United States. Russian actions only succeeded in creating what the rulers of Russia must fear profoundly: a military and economic organization of most of the Western world designed for no other purpose than to oppose Russian power.

In Europe the effect of Russian action and of American counteraction since 1945 has been to hasten the decay of the traditional nation-state organization of the Continent.

This decay antedated World War II; some of its aspects antedated World War I, despite the fact that nationalism seemed to win its culminating triumphs with the Versailles peace settlement. In eastern Europe, where nationalism and the formation of nation-states were a recent growth, the small and mutually hostile states which emerged from World War I proved quite incapable of solving the economic and military problems which faced them. The inescapable facts of geography placed these states between two great powers, Germany and Russia, and they could exist independently only as long as neither the one nor the other chose to attack. A second and almost equally important weakness was that the newborn countries of eastern Europe suffered from rural poverty and overpopulation and scarcely escaped from economic depression at any time between the wars. As a result, discontent became endemic, and in 1944 and 1945 this discontent provided the Russians with a considerable amount of popular support for the revolution from above which the Red Army brought in its wake.

In western Europe, where the nation-states were larger, richer, and more firmly rooted in the past, the failure of the traditional form of political organization has been almost equally complete. Militarily, it is no longer possible for countries like France and Britain to stand alone against such overwhelming power as either Russia or the United States could bring against them. Economically, the decay of western Europe is a complicated process, arising partly from social traditions and institutions which interfere with the most rational employment of resources, partly from a standard of living and leisure which some other peoples do not expect, partly from depletion of indigenous raw materials, partly from capital destruction and obsolescence, and partly from the loss of dominion over parts of the colonial world which once supplied raw materials and markets for European industry and profitable fields for investment to European capitalists. Factors such as these have combined to weaken the economy of western Europe in comparison with newer industrial areas of the world;[2] and the weakness of their economies makes it impossible for the western European nations to support the cost of military establishments adequate to provide for their security without assistance from outside.

The contemporary decay of national sovereignty in Europe conforms to a pattern that has twice before appeared in European history. In the time of Philip and Alexander of Macedon, the Greek city-states found themselves rather suddenly confronted with a comparatively vast and overwhelmingly powerful kingdom; and for more than a century after Alexander's death the old center of Hellenic civilization lost effective political independence and became instead the principal theater for a struggle between the rulers of Egypt and of Macedon. Again, at the end of the fifteenth century A.D., the city-states of northern Italy, which had been the seats of the brilliant civilization of the Renaissance, experienced a similar fate when the king-

2. This is not to say that in absolute terms European wealth has declined. Indeed, most indexes of production show that European mines and factories are producing more than ever before; but the rate of growth is less than in the United States or Russia. Moreover, the expansion of European production was vastly helped by American credits, without which recovery from the war could not have occurred so rapidly and completely as it did.

doms of France and Spain rather abruptly intervened in their affairs and for more than a century struggled intermittently for control and influence in the Italian peninsula.

In both these cases the power of the new giant states arose in good part from the adaptation of techniques of government and military organization which had first been developed in the civilized centers of the day. Thus Philip of Macedon and his successors adapted and improved Greek military tactics, and the rulers of the Hellenistic kingdoms based their power on Greek administrators and upon a Greek type of city organization which they planted, after Alexander's example, in the matrix of oriental or barbarian societies. Similarly, in the sixteenth century A.D., imitation and adaptation of Italian administrative and economic methods underpinned the new strength of the French and Spanish national monarchies. In particular, the kings began to hire professional troops and to maintain them as a standing army after the example first set by Italian cities and principalities.

It is obvious that the contemporary rise of Russian and American world power is a direct result of their adaptation of a pattern of industrial society which first grew up in western Europe. Indeed, from this point of view, the contemporary plight of the old and famous nation-states of Europe seems very like the plight of Greek and Italian city-states in times gone by. There is, of course, an obvious difference of scale. It is not cities but nations that are today undergoing political eclipse; demicontinents, not nations, are today rising in power.

There is also a more important qualitative difference. Macedon in the fourth and third centuries B.C. and France and Spain in the sixteenth century A.D. were participants in a civilization whose center was the Greek and the Italian city-states, respectively. The United States bears the same relationship to western Europe in our own time; but the position of the Soviet Union is not so simple. Russian society is not a daughter of the West in the sense that American society is. Something approximating a distinct civilization, with an outlook of its own and with institutions and traditions of its own, existed in Muscovy before Peter the Great (1689–1725) opened wide the door to the West. After Peter's time the Russian peoples long remained awkwardly on the threshold, half within and half without the pale of Western civilization. The Bolsheviks, however, seem to have made a change. Despite a massive introduction of Western technology during the past thirty-six years, no one would be inclined to argue that Russia was more like the West in 1953 than it had been in 1917. Indeed, the Bolsheviks took a Western creed as well as Western machinery and swallowed them, like a double vodka, neat. The effect was exhilarating, not to say intoxicating. Under Stalin both ideology and technology were tellingly used as weapons against the West, while at home elements of the czarist tradition were revived or maintained with a new vigor and self-confidence.

Thus the new political constellation of the world, pitting America against Russia, also pits one civilization against a variant so strong as almost to constitute a rival civilization. In the nineteenth and earlier centuries, when western European dominance extended over most of the globe, the rival nation-states of Europe constituted a community. They all accepted a very similar outlook upon the world and operated within similar institutional frameworks. Just because European states shared common attitudes and institutions to such a grèat extent, their diplomatic and military relations resembled the behavior of the bits of colored glass in a kaleidoscope. Shifts in the balance could produce new alignments and alliances from time to time; but moves always took place within restraining walls which gave a pattern and cohesion to the political maneuvers and to the military actions of the constituent states.

World Wars I and II broke through the conventional limits which had formerly restrained the states of the European community. Far more tenuous, far less dependable bonds unite the Soviet Union with the United States than formerly united France, Germany, Britain, Austria, and Russia with one another. Instead of a world dominated by a single though internally divided center, our postwar world finds itself torn between two great agglomerations of power, each of which represents a form of society so divergent from the other as to make mutual understanding—not to say trust—difficult if not impossible.[3]

3. More will be said below of the contemporary conflict between Western and non-Western civilizations and of the peculiar place the Soviet Union occupies in that conflict. Here it is enough to suggest that analogous conflicts are not lacking in history. Indeed, the relation of Ptolemaic Egypt to Greece in the two centuries after Alexander's death was in more than one respect similar to Russia's contemporary relationship to western Europe. The Ptolemies were able to graft Greek civilization onto an Egyptian stem, and this combination supported a very powerful state for a few generations. The economic policy of the Ptolemies curiously approximated the state socialism of Stalin's Russia, and Ptolemaic military policy, seeking to influence or control the cities of Greece itself, can be compared with that attempted by the Soviet Union in Europe since 1945.

Had the Spain of Ferdinand and Isabella accepted the Moslems and Jews

We are, therefore, experiencing not only a change in scale but also a change in the quality of interstate relations; and, for reasons we have already seen, the two great rivals are not content to scowl across the world at one another but instead seek actively to mobilize under their leadership the resources of the other states and peoples of the earth. The struggle is world wide. Events in every part of the earth react upon the balance between the two supranational organizations of power, and the competition between the two leading states profoundly affects the "domestic" affairs of every nation and people. What once could with some accuracy be called "foreign affairs" have therefore really ceased to be foreign. Instead, they affect and sometimes dominate the domestic policies and actions of nearly every state in the world, large and small alike.

The division of the industralized portions of the earth between the Russian and the American sphere became fairly definite by 1949. It seems unlikely that any great change (short of the outbreak of a new world war) will come in the boundaries so drawn through Europe and the Far East. Possession of industrial power is clearly recognized by all participants as the key to military strength, and, rather than see any important industrial region pass from one to the other side, the potential loser might be expected to resort to any measure, including war.

The division of the regions of the earth which are predominantly agrarian has not gone so far. Important regions

---

into some sort of partnership instead of expelling them from the country, the Spanish kingdom might have played an analogous "hybrid" role vis-à-vis the Italian city-states in the sixteenth century. But such neat historical parallelism is denied us by the facts of the case.

of southern and eastern Asia have not definitely been annexed to either camp, and such extensive portions of the earth as Africa and South America have very weak and imperfect links with the free world.

Indeed, one of the major themes of contemporary international politics is the struggle between Russia and the United States for influence over the agrarian, relatively undeveloped portions of the earth. The peoples of these countries do not belong irrevocably to either camp; and one reason for this fact is that very real and profound cleavages exist between their economic interests and those of industrialized societies of whatever political hue.

3

The Economic Cleavage.—It is obvious that the interests of countries which produce food and industrial raw materials for export are not the same as the interests of countries which buy these products and sell manufactured goods in exchange. This simple economic opposition is a case of the age-old conflict between farmer and townsman and is comparable to the collision of interest between employer and wage-earner within industrialized society. In all these conflicts it is a difficult matter to strike a balance which will be accepted as fair by both sides. Even within a single political framework the contrary pressure of farmers and of consumers, or of workmen and of employers, is hard to adjudicate. When there is no common political authority which can mediate and, if need be, compel agreement, the conflict becomes doubly difficult.

In the nineteenth century, European economists argued that all such apparent conflicts of interest could be adjusted fairly by the free play of market prices. Practice never entirely conformed to this theory; and in recent times, when government trading has become a very important element in international exchanges, the field within which market prices have a more or less untrammeled play has been reduced much further. Thus British purchases of Persian oil or of Argentine beef have become matters of political negotiation between governments, as have American purchases of Malayan tin or of uranium ore from the Belgian Congo. Under circumstances such as these there is no real free market to set prices on an impersonal, neutral basis. This is even more completely true of the monopolistic state trading that characterizes Russian economic transactions with other Communist countries.

The intervention of government officials in international trade has the effect of transforming economic into political negotiation. Haggling over prices becomes an affair not between individuals or firms but between nations and governments; and a new range of motives comes into play. National pride, military calculation, party maneuvers within one or another of the trading countries—any of these may determine the outcome of a particular trade negotiation. Even if cool calculation of economic gain should chance to dominate both parties to a negotiation, the short-run collision of interest between supplier and purchaser becomes more obvious and difficult when governments trade than is the ease when large numbers of private firms engage in international trading, for in the latter situation changes in price appear as private gain or loss rather than as a national affront or windfall.

Quarrels over the terms of trade between industrial and

agrarian countries is, however, a relatively superficial, even if a troublesome, cleavage between two halves of the world. Much more pervasive is the fact that the socio-economic problems of the earth's peasant millions and their general outlook upon the world differ radically from those of the industrial millions. Let me try to explain.

One may argue that the greatest problem facing industrial societies today is the over-all human adjustment to the new way of life for which mass production in factories provides the material basis. These problems are manifold. There is the matter of distributing purchasing power within industrialized communities in such a fashion as to assure a stable market. There is the matter of co-ordination and control of production, from the getting of raw materials to the distribution of finished products. There is the matter of striking a humanly satisfactory balance between the routine of factory labor and the activities of leisure time. And, overriding all, there is the matter of how to blend the contradictory ends to which industrial production may be directed: whether to make it serve the wants of individual consumers (if so, what wants?) or whether to put the collective strength of the industrial community first (i.e., build armaments and train men to use them).

Generally speaking, these problems are not genuinely soluble within the framework of existing political institutions. Certainly they are not soluble within the restricted territories of the nation-states of Europe. Europeans can no longer control satisfactorily the flow of raw materials from abroad or assure themselves of foreign markets for their goods, yet modern industrial society depends for its existence on exchanges which in Europe's case have to traverse political frontiers. Larger states such as the Soviet Union and the United States could, perhaps, create something very close to an autarkic industrial community within their political boundaries. But such an achievement would involve very real damage to economic efficiency, and autarky would do nothing to solve the greatest problem of them all—the collision between welfare and warfare as goals and guides to the industrial process.

Moreover, even with all the levers of economic administration gathered together under one political roof, there is no certainty that the problems of human adjustment to industrialism will be satisfactorily solved. Collisions of interest between various occupational groups within industrial society cannot easily be avoided. Certainly nationalization of industrial enterprises does not eliminate such collisions, though it may somewhat alter the criteria by which disputes are adjudicated. Laws and regulations together with administrative decisions and calculations, all skilfully backed by persuasion, may do much to adjust the internal frictions of industrial society; but without a fairly definite moral code to guide individual behavior—a code adjusted finely enough to social realities so that expectations and actual results from a given course of action usually coincide in fact—without such a code one must expect that the human relations of industrial society will continue to generate disappointment and discontent among large numbers of men who find themselves subjected to a personally unrewarding routine.

If we restrict our attention to the more immediate problems of industrial society and ask ourselves how the two political halves of the world attempt to meet them, it becomes obvious at once that the Russians are both more logical and more inhumane than we.

Despite the liberal—indeed, anarchic—vision of an ultimate Communist society which remains at the center of Marxian doctrine, the Bolsheviks elected to subordinate welfare to warfare as the short-run guide to their economic policy. From their inception in 1928, the five-year plans put the development of heavy industry ahead of the development of light industry; and since about 1934 it seems correct to say that the first call upon the newly created heavy industry was the production of armaments.[4] As a result of this policy, the standard of living of the ordinary Russian has probably risen little if at all under the Bolsheviks, while the military strength of the Soviet state has multiplied many times over.

The problem of how to distribute purchasing power in order to assure a steady market became, under the Soviet system, a calculation of how much of the total national resources could be assigned to capital development and military consumption without seriously interfering with the morale and productivity of the civilian working force. Given a chronic shortage of civilian goods, it was usually not difficult to sop up any surplus cash which might have come into private hands by putting special goods on sale

4. Just as this page was leaving my hands, Premier Malenkov announced in August, 1953, a new emphasis upon consumer goods for the coming year. It is too soon to say whether this will turn out to be an enduring change of policy. Once before, in 1932, priority for consumer goods was officially announced only to be abandoned within a few months under the threat of increasing danger from outside.

at fantastically high prices. The difficulty was, rather, to find the goods.

The problem of co-ordination and control of the industrial process became for the Bolsheviks a problem of administration, of planning and priorities, of manpower and material allocations, of production goals and norms.[5] The problem of balancing the routine of the factory with leisure-time activities became largely a problem of political indoctrination.

One may doubt how satisfactory the result of these practices may be from the point of view of the ordinary Russian citizen. There is every reason to believe that most Russians lead strenuous and bleak lives, deprived of some of the material goods which in Western countries have come to be considered indispensable even for the poorest classes. But the power of police and propaganda makes whatever discontent there is inarticulate.

5. It is a striking fact that the war economies which were developed during World War II by all the major belligerents paralleled many of the economic methods the Russians have used since 1928. Governmental control over economic life was, of course, more pervasive in the Soviet Union than it ever became in Britain or America, and methods differed greatly in detail. But likenesses were surprisingly great. Not production for profit but production for governmental order; not free access to raw materials and component parts for any purchaser ready to pay the price but a system of priorities and allocations entitling each factory to a share of the available supplies; not production for the individual consumer but production for the wants of some organization, whether a new factory or army, navy, and air force. These characteristics of the Bolshevik economy were all paralleled in the war economies of Britain, America, Germany, and Japan.

To put the matter in another way, one may argue that Bolshevik economic administration was a development of war economy carried over into peacetime. Or perhaps one should not accuse real Bolsheviks of making peace with a capitalist world and should rather say that their policy makes economic mobilization normal.

It seems clear that the Russians have purchased collective military might at a very high price. Vast suffering has been systematically inflicted on millions of Russians, and serious deprivation has been visited upon them all. Against this must be set the psychological *élan* which comes to a people whose industrial and national power is expanding rapidly. The sense of having embarked upon a great undertaking— the industrialization and modernization of Russia—sustains the Bolsheviks and is undoubtedly shared by many Russians who are not members of the party. The conviction that the Bolshevik pattern of industrial society is the best, most just, most efficient, and most in accord with the nature of things is also an important element in Russian psychology. While imitating the West in technique, many, perhaps a great many, Russians believe that they have improved the organization of industrial society by substituting their version of socialism for the Western brand of capitalism.

The non-Communist industrial nations lack the harsh, clear-cut answers to all problems which (at least from the outside) seem to be characteristic of the Bolshevik regime. Uneasy compromise between production for war and production for civilian consumption prevails today in western Europe and in the United States. Uneasy compromise between state control of industrial production and control by private corporations is matched by an inexact and perhaps undependable adjustment between purchasing power and the supply of goods. Nor can one say that a satisfactory adjustment between work and leisure activity has been widely established among the industrial workingmen of Western nations.

The absence of clear-cut solutions to these problems

may, one hopes, make for greater flexibility in Western society—a flexibility that may compensate for the public and private friction which it clearly permits and, perhaps, encourages. The apparent solidarity of Russian society almost certainly hides deep dissatisfactions, and it is not inconceivable that some day the Russian people may turn savagely upon their present rulers just as in 1917 they turned upon the officials and officers who served the czar. However deep the conflicts within Western society, the very fact that they get a daily airing in the public press prevents any secret, subterranean accumulation of resentment such as probably is occurring in Russia.

But, no matter how comforting we may find speculations about potential Russian weakness, the very existence of the Bolshevik government and its control of the manpower and other resources of a large part of the earth presents the Western world with a pressing immediate problem of deciding how to divide attention between welfare and warfare. In the short run the question is one of how to divide factory production and manpower between military and civilian pursuits; and this is difficult enough when the intentions and real military strength of the Russians and of their allies can only be guessed. In the longer run, however, even more serious problems arise. The whole structure of Western society, with the standard and ideals of Western civilization, is, or threatens to fall into, a vast melting pot. In an age when conscious control of social institutions and attitudes has acquired an unprecedented scope and power, preparation for war, if carried to a logical extreme, must transform society into a garrison, poised to parry attack and to administer devastating counterattack.

In proportion as Bolshevik Russia approaches the condition of a garrison state, the pressure upon Western nations to do likewise becomes stronger. Yet so to imitate our rival would involve a fundamental and far from admirable self-transformation. The dilemma, however, is real. Few would voluntarily and deliberately choose to subject themselves to Russian power, yet a policy of pursuing welfare to the neglect of warfare would very likely have that unintended result. Relatively large military forces, capable of deterring or if need be of repelling Communist attack, are surely needed if the Western world is long to remain its own master. Yet such forces will inevitably affect the social texture of American and European society, and, the larger they become, the deeper and more indelible will be their imprint.

It is obvious that the demands of military discipline accord ill with the frame of mind which values individual human lives and emphasizes individual rights against official authority. In war soldiers are asked to sacrifice themselves for some extra-personal group, whether the platoon, the division, or the country as a whole; they are further asked to obey the commands of superiors without question and without hesitation. The transition from a society professing respect for the individual and exalting the common man to an army in which the individual soldier is ideally no more than a replaceable part in a great machine is not an easy one. By contrast, Russian civilian relationships are generally conformable to the military pattern: authority and compulsion and unquestioning obedience to superiors and indifference to the wishes of subordinates characterize

Russian administration.[6] For an ordinary Soviet citizen it is probably the case that to get into the army in time of peace is a positive relief. There he may find better food and clothing, and win greater social prestige, while the hardships and irritations of barracks life probably no more than equal those which beset civilians.

The opposition which exists between the traditional liberal values of Western industrial society and the military virtues needed to preserve political independence is a major problem for the United States and for western Europe. The long-range outcome will depend upon the future course of international events. It is not inconceivable that two or three generations of cold war, punctuated, perhaps, by a series of localized military clashes such as that fought in Korea in 1950–53, might in time turn Western society into a militarized simulacrum of Russia. Such an outcome would involve the loss of much that is most precious and distinctive in Western civilization. The possibility of such a loss is one of the great dangers of our time.

In thinking about the difficulties now confronting industrial society, it is always worth reminding ourselves how very recent, historically speaking, is the rise of industrialism. After all, the daily lives of hundreds of millions of men have been radically transformed within the past four or five generations, and the transformation still continues as industrialism spreads to new ground and as new methods of production and transport arise within older industrial socie-

6. This is not an accident. The czarist state did its best to militarize Russian society, for only by so doing could it compete successfully with strong and threatening neighbors—first from the steppe, later from the west. Communist militarism is inspired by the same sort of fear.

ties. One must expect that such massive changes in individual lives will promote radical changes in social and political relations between men. We ought not to be surprised, therefore, that men living under newfangled and extremely complicated circumstances should not yet have been able to arrive at any stable or satisfactory adjustment to the comparatively very new requirements of industrial living.

The economic problems which confront contemporary agrarian societies are profoundly different from those confronting industrial nations. In more than half the earth the overriding problem today is how to bring population into better balance with the developed resources of the land. In India, China, Japan, Southeast Asia, in the Middle East, in southern and eastern Europe, and, less pressingly, in South America and in Africa, the recent growth of population has outstripped the development of resources by which the people may live. Subdivision of farms or peasant holdings among a numerous progeny can solve the problem only for a generation or two: when farms become too small to support a family in bad seasons, periodic famine becomes inevitable, and miserable poverty becomes normal.

This is not the place to attempt an exploration of the reasons for the astounding growth of population in the agrarian parts of the world. A lowered death rate, resulting in part at least from the introduction of more effective medical treatment, is usually held responsible; but population growth seems to continue under conditions of very precarious life, and accurate information about birth and death rates in older times is so scanty that comparison between present and former conditions must be largely speculative.

The fact remains that human population is growing by the million year after year in regions of the earth where there are no adequate means of livelihood for the new inhabitants. A vicious circle exists, for, as population begins to outstrip the development of new resources, it becomes more and more difficult to check the disbalance. Poverty-stricken peasants find it harder and harder to introduce new methods of farming that might bring higher yields from their land. Even such elementary improvements as the use of fertilizer may easily become too expensive for the peasant farmer to afford; and, being unable to afford such things, his poverty simply becomes deeper. Larger works of capital improvement—drainage, water control, etc.—are even more definitely beyond the resources of the individual farmer, and the collective accumulation of capital to pay for such improvements becomes very difficult when the population as a whole is living at or near the subsistence level.

Industrialization—often considered a sovereign cure for rural overpopulation—is hampered by the same difficulty. How, in an impoverished country, can new factories be paid for when every scrap of food is needed to keep the existing population alive? There are two possible answers. One is foreign loans, coming from the richer and already industrialized parts of the world. But such loans are likely to involve political dependence and often involve economic tribute in the form of interest payments as well. Such dependence has become more and more distasteful to agrarian peoples.

The other possibility open to agrarian countries is to force capital accumulation at home by government policy. This was the path the Bolsheviks took, and Russia's example has become a potent magnet to all the backward parts of the earth as a result. In effect the Bolsheviks were able to raise Russia within a generation from its traditional role as an agrarian nation into a great industrial and world power. This was done by brutally taking food from the peasants and using it, among other things, to feed men who worked at building new factories and at turning out goods from factories already built. More than once the policy of the Bolshevik state brought famine and hunger to millions of peasant households; and up to the present (1953) the peasants of Russia never received a supply of industrial goods and services that came near to equaling the value (when measured by Western rates of exchange) of the grain and other foodstuffs taken from them.

But the Russians had some special advantages in undertaking their forced-draft industrialization. In the first place, they had abundant raw materials and great spaces of only partially developed land. In parts of czarist Russia, to be sure, rural overpopulation had become a pressing problem; but there were other parts, especially in the east, where potentially fertile acres lay waiting the plow. Hence it was not difficult to adjust population to resources when force was used to move millions to the undeveloped parts of the Soviet Union, and when millions more were attracted or conscripted to work in industry or assigned to build new factories, railroads, etc.

Whether countries like India or China could successfully imitate the Russian model is unsure. Their peasant millions are even more numerous than the Russian millions; undeveloped land is scarcer than in Russia; the margin of starvation is a good deal closer to most Indian and Chinese peasants than it was to the Russian peasants—or, put in the converse fashion, the surplus agricultural production of the great Asian nations is smaller. After all, Russia had been a major exporter of grain before the Bolshevik revolution—proof of the fact that a considerable margin between production and minimal rural food consumption existed. No comparable surplus of food is produced in either China or India today. It follows that an effort to industrialize either nation as rapidly as Russia industrialized herself without loans from abroad would involve greater suffering and perhaps the starvation of millions.

No easy and sure solution of the economic problems which press so insistently upon the agrarian nations can be seen. Just as the problems of industrial societies can hardly be solved within existing political boundaries, so, too, it seems improbable that the major agrarian countries can surmount their difficulties by withdrawing inside their own frontiers in order to direct their effort to rapid capital development on a scale necessary to provide the means of livelihood for the millions of new mouths born each year.

Before a more nearly stable and satisfactory economic balance can be achieved between population and resources, profound changes will be necessary in the habits, attitudes, and occupations of the peasant peoples of the earth. Such changes are sure to prove painful, and it may well be doubted whether they will come without violence. Yet, if changes are not made, one can be sure that the traditional cures for overdense peasant population will once more come into play, and overpopulation will be relieved in the age-old way by outbreaks of famine, pestilence, and war.

The fact that the great problems confronting industrial societies are so dissimilar to those confronting agrarian societies makes a vast difference in the points of view of the two halves of the world—a difference which does nothing to smooth over the direct clash of economic interest between the suppliers and the purchasers of raw materials and foodstuffs. Yet these economic cleavages are less to the forefront of men's minds than are either the political divisions of the earth, which we have already considered, or the cultural and racial antagonisms, which we must consider next. The deepest emotional and irrational roots of human nature attach themselves more directly to the color of a man's skin and to his manners and customs than to the less apparent economic oppositions and divergences. In helping to shape the future, the noise of clashing states, ideologies, races, and civilizations seems likely to obscure the quieter action of strictly economic circumstances.

Yet any effort to look steadily into the future should, I think, take seriously into account the conditions under which industrialism is most likely to flourish. Just because men so generally desire the goods which industrial production can make available to them, it will in the long run be much easier to win general assent to a world system that gives industrialism the fullest possible scope than it would be to win assent for some other arrangement of world society. And, without the assent of most of the living generation of mankind, no system of world society is likely to endure for long. Hence it seems unlikely that anything ap-

nating a stable political, social, and economic world
r will be established which does not allow the widest
ope to industrial production and exchange.

4

The Cultural and Racial Cleavage.—The contemporary
form of world racial and cultural relations is mainly a
consequence of the extraordinary expansion of European
power and influence which occurred between the sixteenth
and nineteenth centuries. During these centuries Europeans
enjoyed a secure technical superiority over the other peoples of the earth, and, being stronger, they were tempted to
treat natives of other climes with scant consideration. The
occasional philosophic admiration for the noble savage of
America or for the sages of China seldom affected the attitudes and behavior of the soldiers, merchants, missionaries,
and adventurers who actually came into contact with the
other peoples of the world. Alien civilizations usually
struck such Europeans as heathen superstition, and they
often treated the colored races as lesser breeds without the
law.

Particularly in Asia, where old and complex civilizations
had existed long before Europeans appeared on the scene,
the haughty white man excited resentment which in our
own time is coming to political expression more clearly
and powerfully than at any time in the past. In the nineteenth century the indisputable fact that Europeans were
militarily more powerful and able economically to produce
cheap and useful machine-made goods paralyzed all but
desperate and sporadic efforts to repel their encroachment;
but, in proportion as Western techniques and ideas have

found foothold, Asians have gained both the means and the will to resist and to throw off European dominance.

Yet successful resistance requires extensive reorganization within the Asian societies themselves. Generally speaking, Asian leaders wish to do two more or less incompatible things: to adopt Western industrial technology and thus make their countries rich and powerful and yet to preserve the traditions of their own civilization against the rude encroachment of alien ideas and attitudes from the West. A profound ambivalence toward Western civilization results. On the one hand, the West provides a model for imitation and admiration; on the other, it represents the enemy against which every effort must be turned in order to restore the dignity and greatness of the past.

This ambivalence runs through all the relations between the Western industrialized world and the rest of mankind. The Moslem peoples of the Middle East share it with peoples of Asia; Latin-Americans exhibit a similar, if less extreme, ambivalence in their relations with the United States. In Africa the Negroes have only begun to stir against European dominance, but, in proportion as a group of leaders educated to a familiarity with Western ideas and techniques arises among them, it seems certain that a similar mixture of attraction and repulsion will take hold among African peoples also.

The old civilizations and peoples of the world are reasserting themselves against the white man's West, after having borrowed enough from Western civilization to make the rejection of white domination practicable. The revolt of Asia and of Islam is a passionate, violent movement. Its leaders are driven more by their feelings than by their reason—feelings which arise from a profound and powerful human impulse.

It is certainly unfortunate but nonetheless true that antipathies between peoples of different civilization and physical appearance are more than idle prejudice to be laughed away. Antipathies of this sort are fed by the deepest social instincts. Human societies have in the past been able to exist only by persuading their members to cling to what is familiar and to reject as far as possible all things alien; and, in any case of quarrel with an outsider, the first impulse is always to support one's fellow against his enemy, regardless of the rights or wrongs of the case. Thus the very social instincts which maintain a modicum of harmony within a society automatically tend to pit it against alien communities.

The efforts of individuals to bridge the gap between alien civilizations are therefore beset with pitfalls. Even with the best will in the world, subtle barriers separate persons whose minds and feelings are attuned to divergent ways of life. Nuances of feeling and meaning are missed, which mean that misunderstanding in greater or less degree is always present in any personal contact; and this failure of understanding may easily flare up into hostility whenever one or the other person falls back upon his identification with his own people and abandons the effort to penetrate into the alien world of the other.

The obstacles to personal sympathy across cultural barriers are vastly increased when marked differences of outward appearance become the symbols of cultural differences and a basis for social discrimination. In mixed societies, where men of different race and culture live side by side, it normally happens that each group draws a sort of invisible curtain around itself, recognizing as friends and equals only persons of the same physical appearance and cultural background. Under such circumstances, even very small differences—differences more of bearing and manner than of physiology sometimes—may serve to delimit the circles of social solidarity and sympathy.[7]

Every complex society presents analogous divergencies among classes, professions, religious groups, etc. Such groups regularly develop a more or less definite ethos which marks them off from full equality and sympathy with others. But, when differences of ethos are published to the world by outward differences of appearance, the effect is like that achieved by wearing military badges of rank. Personal relations between a general and a private can never be those of man to man, simple and easy, even if by chance the two should be friends. In any such situation rank will always hover in the background of consciousness and obtrude a sense of awkwardness. The same thing happens when racial badges separate individuals, and, even when (as in the case of American whites and Negroes) there are no great differences in habits, standards, and moral ideas to divide the races, no mere argument can eliminate the psychological reality of the barrier between them.

It is an interesting and disturbing fact that the antipathy between the major races of mankind involves the sense of smell. Chinese, for example, regard the smell of white men in much the same light as many whites regard the smell of

7. The social status of Jews in eastern Europe shows how a physically almost indistinguishable population may yet retain its separateness over a period of generations and centuries.

Negroes: animal rankness. The differences in smell are real enough, whether they arise from differences in diet, cleanliness, or other cause; and the fact that men notice and react to such differences puts racial relations under the influence of a very primitive sense—one much closer to our instinctual equipment than is the finer, more rationalized sense of sight.

Obviously the practical force and direction of racial and cultural antipathies depends very much upon the size of the grouping to which men give their loyalty and the groups which they regard as alien. Until fairly recently, taking world history as a whole, attachments to local and personal groups far outweighed all others. The village community, family, or tribe counted for vastly more than any larger association. This is still the case in important parts of the world—among the Negroes of Africa, for example, and (it seems likely) among most of the people of India and China as well.

Over a period of centuries, and most rapidly during the past one hundred and fifty years, Europeans were persuaded to expand their concept of community to embrace a nationality, often but not always conceived as being co-terminal with an existing state. When this occurred, men could cease regarding rulers and officials as fundamentally alien beings, whose demands for taxes and services were inescapable evils. Instead they could and did identify themselves and their community with the nation-state.

The political transformations of Europe in the nineteenth and twentieth centuries would have been inconceivable without such a transfer of loyalty from locality to nationality. Whenever the limits of state and nationality coincided or could easily be made to coincide, the advantages which derived from the transfer of loyalty to a larger unit were very great, both in the military and in the economic sphere. Conversely, where state and nationality boundaries did not coincide, the new spirit led to internal weakness and, in time of crisis, to paralysis and upheaval.

In the parts of the world where European types of society have come to exist, nationality remains the largest unit to which men normally attach their loyalty. But it is no longer only European peoples that have experienced and are experiencing a transfer of loyalty to new and larger social units. In some parts of the non-European world, for example, in the Arab countries of the Middle East, the patterns of a new nationalism seem to be following a path substantially like that first worked out in Europe itself. In the two great nations of Asia, however, the social unit to which local loyalties are in process of transfer is quite different. It is as though Europeans had elected to adhere to Christendom rather than to separate nationalities; and to use the European term "nationalism" to describe what is happening in India and China is perhaps more harmful than helpful to clear thinking. The "nationalism" of Indian and of Chinese intellectuals and officials unites or attempts to unite an entire racial and cultural stem of mankind. In so doing, it overleaps barriers of language and of geography comparable to those which in Europe led to the rise of separate and rival nationalisms.

To be sure, the change in human loyalties among the peoples of Asia has not yet percolated very far down the social scale. It is altogether likely that a majority of the peasants of both India and China persist in their old attitude toward political affairs, passively distrusting officials and clinging to the more familiar, dependable, and traditional loyalty to family, village community, and, in India's case, caste. Yet among the educated minority which is the bearer of the new Asian "nationalism," identification of culture, race, and "nationality" has been firmly implanted. Even when Hindu or Chinese populations have migrated overseas, the feeling that they inalienably belong to the home country is very strong.

The fate of the Chinese warlords and of European concessionaires who for so long distracted the political life of China illustrates the power that the new Asian attitude of mind can exercise in organizing political transformation; and the manner in which the princely states of India collapsed when confronted with the demands of the Indian government in 1947 shows just as clearly how this new attitude can break through and erase old institutions. The combination of Asian "nationalism" and the world-wide revolt against the West which it organizes makes a tremendously powerful force. Together with the clash between the Soviet and the American state systems, the Asian *risorgimento* seems likely to dominate the history of the world in the next century.

As in so many other respects, the Soviet Union occupies a peculiar place in the racial and cultural conflicts which presently divide mankind. Russians long disputed whether they should conceive themselves as the easternmost outpost of European civilization or whether they were really a separate people, whose historic task was to preserve their own peculiar heritage against the encroachment of the West. The Russian attitude toward the West was and remains very similar to the repulsion-attraction which so distracts the non-European societies of the earth. Like the peoples of Asia, many Russians wish to imitate Western technology (and to surpass it); yet at the same time they wish to retain their peculiarity, their separateness. The Bolshevik movement was once thoroughly "Western" in its orientation. Lenin thought his revolution would be part of a European revolt against capitalism, and he both despised and regretted Russian backwardness (i.e., Russian differences from the leading countries of western Europe). Yet, oddly enough, the fact that the revolution stopped short at Russia's frontiers by degrees allowed the transformation of bolshevism into a creed bitterly opposed to the West and all its works. Stalin became a true heir of the Slavophiles of the nineteenth century. Like them, he sought to preserve and cultivate Russia's peculiarity; and, like them, he proudly claimed a messianic future for the Russian way of life. It is still too soon to say what may be the policy of Stalin's successors, but it is hard to see what would persuade them to change a formula that has won such resounding success in the recent past.

Obviously, the likeness between Russian reaction to Western civilization and that of Asian peoples establishes a certain bond of sympathy. In another respect, too, Russia can hope to appeal to the Asians. There are millions of Mongols, Turkomen, and other non-European races in the Soviet Union, and the Bolsheviks made a special point of treating, or pretending to treat, these peoples as the equals of the Great Russians. The further fact that the Russians can point to their success in transforming an agrarian into a powerful industrial society gives them still another advantage, for the Russians have done what nearly all Asian leaders would like to do. To many educated, sensitive, and intelligent men—men very much alive to the ambiguities and difficulties of their present relation with white men from the West—it seems obvious that the Russian example is the one to follow.[8]

There is, however, another side to Russian national psychology, which, when allowed to manifest itself, repels foreign sympathies. The very ambivalence the Russians seem to show in their relationship to the West implies a partly suppressed sense of inferiority. The inner insecurity which results may encourage (and in fact has produced) blustering self-glorification—a sort of national egotism which easily turns into a harsh imperialism. In eastern and central Europe, for example, where the Russians have recently enjoyed political dominance, it seems clear that they have alienated the support of almost the entire population. Their airs of superiority, their economic exploitation, their forcible repression of all nationalistic or other

8. There is, I suggest, an important difference between Communists in Western countries and those of non-Western parts of the world. In proportion as international communism came under the direction of Moscow and became anti-Western, its adherents in the West came to be recruited more and more from a group of nihilistic revolutionaries whose dominant characteristic was a sweeping, blind, and destructive rejection of the society into which they had been born. But in Asia and perhaps in other parts of the non-Western world, to be a Communist does not necessarily involve rejection of ancestral values in quite the same way; indeed, Communist revolution is attractive to many because it seems to offer a short cut to power and independence—power with which to rebuff the intrusive white men and thus win full independence to develop ancestral traditions.

dissent, and the arbitrary behavior of Russian officials have all offended the feelings of satellite populations. Whether the Russians will be more successful in China, and will be able to create an easy comradeship and sense of solidarity with the Communist rulers of that country, remains a question of the greatest significance for the future. On the face of things, it seems most unlikely that Russo-Chinese friction can be avoided; but, as long as the Chinese see a greater enemy in the United States and in European imperialism, it is unlikely that such friction will find overt expression.

Yet, whatever their shortcomings, it remains true that the Russians, simply by virtue of their peculiar relation to the West, have a great advantage in appealing for the support of the majority of mankind. In the racial and cultural conflict which divides that majority from white and Western man, the Russians, though undeniably white, can at least claim to be against the West and to have given the first example of how to turn Western weapons against the West. The United States, by comparison, suffers from being the heir, in fact if not in form, of European imperialism. This is a grave handicap which only great wisdom, restraint, and, one may add, extraordinary luck can overcome or neutralize.

5

The Moral Dimension.—The political, economic, and cultural antagonisms which divide the world are both serious and spectacular. There is, however, still another dimension to our difficulties which may be less apparent but is no less important than the others. In all the world, moral and religious systems are today undergoing very serious strain and threaten still more radical breakdown. I believe that this moral upheaval arises mainly from the unprecedented rate at which habits, customs, and institutions have been and continue to be altered; and this in turn arises partly from a new intensity of contact between alien peoples and civilizations but more basically from the practice of applying deliberate ingenuity to the transformation of military, political, economic, and social affairs.

Until relatively recently, nearly all men accepted the social landscape into which they were born as something established by divine authority which should not be tampered with by any mere mortal. In periods of rapid social changes or partial breakdown of ancestral ways, men were led to wonder, and to question the eternal and permanent nature of their institutions. The *Dialogues* of Plato stand as a magnificent monument to one such period of questioning; but Plato's vision of a city ruled by philosophers—a city whose institutions would be shaped by reason to cultivate the intellectual and moral virtues of an elite while the rest of the inhabitants would be made tractable by the Royal Lie—never became a blueprint for action; and, when Plato tried at Syracuse to translate his principles into practice, he met with dismal failure.

By contrast, in our time the visions of scientists, engineers, and inventors, the ideals of political and economic theorists, the ideas of psychologists and doctors have found the way from theory to practice time and again because businessmen, politicians, administrators, advertisers, and soldiers have seen advantage in the new paths of action suggested by theoreticians. However much such modern ideas may have fallen short of Plato's sweep and grandeur, they have been able to change the daily lives of millions of men drastically and profoundly. Indeed, efforts to increase wealth, to eliminate and cure disease, to create and maintain military power, and to sell new ideas or new products to countless millions have been so successful as to persuade many men, Westerners and non-Westerners alike, that almost any goal can be attained by intelligent effort and appropriate organization.

But there is a contrary and very powerful stream of opinion that runs through the Western world today. Many sensitive people feel blackly pessimistic about the future of humanity. This, I think, may largely be attributed to the decay of religious belief and to the blurring of the moral code which was based upon that belief by our grandfathers. Clearly, religious belief and behavior in accordance with it can do much to relieve both personal and social problems. When a man is convinced that what happens to him personally and to others around him is a part of the working-out of a divine order, then problems of personal choice are simplified, and it becomes easier to endure disappointment or deprivation with equanimity and fortitude. Any seeming injustice can be viewed as working for some larger good, being both a punishment for past sins and a challenge for future betterment. "Whom the Lord loveth, He chasteneth." But in our own time the practical success of those who have tinkered with the traditional order has helped to erode confidence in any direct divine jurisdiction over human affairs. Just because men have so often been successful in deliberately transforming the conditions of their lives, their hopes have turned more and more from salvation in another world to a very different sort of salvation in this.

Such a frame of mind invites people to look for human scapegoats. If men do in fact control their own affairs, at least potentially, then any failure, any personal or collective disappointment, can most easily be explained by attributing it to the stupidity or evil machinations of someone else. This line of argument may, of course, be used by any party to a dispute, and it serves to embitter all forms of social antagonism, both within and between nations. A religious person will at least try to attribute personal disappointments first to his own inadequacy—his sinfulness—and ultimately to God. The ill-will of fellow-men thus becomes a mere instrument in the divine order, providing a punishment, a test, a challenge, or all three at once. Such a frame of mind obviously cushions social conflicts. In times past it has helped to steel individuals to endure hardships and injustices of a sort which are inevitable in a time when traditional ways of life shift so rapidly that familiar habits no longer bring their expected results. Indeed, the view that religion is an indispensable support of society has yet to be disproved. One can argue plausibly that the liberal, democratic society of the West is, in the twentieth century, living upon a humanitarian capital inherited from religious minds of past generations.

The decay of religion has not only sharpened social conflicts; it has also sharpened conflicts within individuals. Without the support of a vivid religious belief and code of ethics based upon that belief, individuals often find themselves profoundly distressed by indecision between alternative courses of action. Put in a different idiom, the customary guides to conduct have lost their sharpness of definition and frequently fail to offer answers to the questions which arise within the lives of individuals or of groups. A pervasive unease results; and with such unease a haunting sense of the futility of human life easily gains sway over men's minds.

Thus both the optimism of those who believe that all things may yet be made new by human will and intelligence and the pessimism of others who feel that the world is getting steadily worse seem to be connected with the extraordinary flux which has come to Western ways of life in the past two or three generations. As old ways have been discarded in favor of new, the whole fabric of Christian belief and the moral code built upon it has, for the most part inadvertently, been shaken. Some rebellious spirits may rejoice in the resultant freedom to chart a new course for themselves and for others; but a majority shiver in their new nakedness and are mightily tempted to search for prophets and teachers who will tell them authoritatively what to believe and what to do with lives that have lost, or threaten to lose, their savor and meaning.

Awareness of their moral difficulties has been growing rapidly among Western intellectuals during the past generation, but in this development the West has lagged far behind other peoples. The rude and sudden impact of Western civilization upon the other civilized (and also uncivilized) peoples of the earth put an extraordinary and infinitely varying strain upon the various moral and religious systems which existed before the onslaught of the West became serious. A part at least of the passivity with which other peoples at first received the European imprint must be attributed to a sort of inner paralysis which gripped the established leaders of the various non-European societies when they first saw the wealth and experienced the power that Europeans could command. Direct imitation of European methods meant a surrender of cherished traditions and attitudes; simple rejection of European ways was impossible because European soldiers, merchants, and missionaries so unmercifully thrust themselves forward and could not long be staved off, even when, as in the case of Japan, a most earnest effort was made to do so.

In our own time the Asian and Moslem peoples are beginning to recover from the catalepsy which the first European impact induced, but it does not appear that any of them has been able to find a moral code or a religion that can assist individuals to achieve peace of mind and at the same time support the solidarity of society and promote or at least tolerate the radical social transformations of our time.

The principal religion in the field is communism; and it has won great victories in Russia and in China and may yet win another victory in India. Communism has certainly been able to attract men's loyalty, transform their lives, and reshape whole societies; but a doctrine which implants class war, cultivates social tensions, and preaches the perfectibility of human society on earth can hardly satisfy mankind for long.

Under present conditions, however, communism is indeed formidable, for it offers men an easy explanation for all the suffering or disappointment they may meet with in life by finding a scapegoat in the form of malignant capitalists and wicked capitalist-imperialist nations.[9] The fact that Communist doctrine has often attracted men of intelligence and sensitivity is one indication of the moral crisis of contemporary societies, both Western and non-Western. Indeed, having first upset the established routine of all the rest of the world, it does not seem fantastic to suggest that the peoples of the West may have raised up their own nemesis. Perhaps their very success in transforming themselves and the world may turn out to have undermined the moral fiber and the social cohesion of the leading nations of the Western world.

Any such analysis as this easily exaggerates. Moralists have been decrying the decay of morals since the dawn of literature. Certainly the majority of men everywhere manage to live out their lives much as usual and are troubled by the moral problems I have attempted to describe only occasionally, perhaps not at all. As long as daily tasks and daily food can be found, most men are glad to leave abstract moral questions strictly alone. Whatever moral crisis exists is therefore only latent and will assume a critical and general importance only in case of some faltering in the routine of daily life. But such faltering has occurred in important parts of the world already. It seems quite likely to do so again and may do so on an even larger scale than before.

9. It is easier to deplore a doctrine which distorts the complexities of truth so irresponsibly and which cultivates men's viler emotions so blatantly than it is to suggest alternatives. To develop a new moral code and a new philosophy or religion capable of supporting men under the tumultuous conditions of life which confront us is today probably beyond human power. Some stabilization, some release from drastic uncertainty and incessant novelty, seems needful before our moral principles and metaphysical ideas can catch up with our practice.

The moral and religious uncertainty of our age is therefore potentially of the highest importance, fully as critical as the political, economic, and cultural antagonisms which are all, in some sense, expressions and embodiments of the moral and religious shortcomings of present (and past) generations.

CHAPTER FOUR

THE FUTURE

1

IF HUMAN AFFAIRS were governed by rational considerations, the first step toward an improvement of the human condition as it prevails today would be the formation of some sort of world political authority; the second step would be to lodge in that authority's hands sufficient military power to make its will enforcible around the globe. Such a political reordering of the world seems an obvious adjustment to the new conditions of human intercourse which have been created since the advent of the epoch of mechanical transport and communication. The destructive effects of unprecedented intimacy of contact between societies situated geographically distant from one another would be minimized by the establishment of a single supreme source of political authority. Indeed, I argued in the preceding chapter that efforts to solve the major problems confronting mankind today cannot gain more than local, temporary, and halting success as long as they must take place within the existing framework of nation-states. This is so primarily because the existing division of the world into a number of separate sovereign states makes war possible; and the possibility of war demands preparation for war, which in turn distracts men's minds, excites their fears, distorts their economies, and fans hostility between races and civilizations. Every major problem confronting us is either created or seriously inflamed by the legacy of old and the possibility of new wars.

The technical feasibility of a world government capable of ending organized international warfare cannot be doubted. Three things would be required: (1) a body of technicians and administrators who would obey some central authority and inform it of what took place on the face of the earth; (2) a monopoly of what might be called "capital" weapons in the hands of an armed force which would obey the orders of a central authority; and, finally, and most necessary of all, (3) a supreme central authority with a will sufficiently firm and united to be able to make decisions and settle disputes among governments and peoples. The techniques of modern administration and the means of communication and transport which men already have at their command would certainly make it possible to maintain the coherence and discipline of a world-wide bureaucracy and of a world-wide army; nor would the cost of maintaining even large numbers of men engaged in such work constitute a prohibitive burden to the people of the earth.

Such a government by its very existence would eliminate the danger of international war as we know it. Bloodshed and violence would not cease, but war involving years of preparation with the mobilization of the energies of millions of men and of the resources of whole continents would come to an end. As long as a supreme central authority maintained a monopoly of capital weapons, no mere nation or even group of nations could hope to defy its decisions with impunity. Instead of relying upon armies and navies to defend their rights and interests, the peoples of the world would have to rely on persuasion, pleading their case before the supreme authority. International conflicts would thus be translated from the military to the legal plane, and the possibility of a more hopeful start toward some solution of the current economic, cultural, and moral difficulties of mankind would begin to open.

World government would involve a considerable loss of national independence and would, in some cases at least, involve extensive interference with cherished national institutions. The decisions of a supreme authority would not please everyone; whole peoples would, on occasion, think them grossly unjust. Especially in international affairs there are many conflicts which cannot be adjudicated without harming the interests or offending the sense of justice of one (sometimes even of both) of the parties. Yet I have no hesitation whatever in asserting that the prompt formation of a world government would be the best and indeed the only rational way to begin trying to meet the difficulties which confront all human societies today.

But how absurd such a picture is! How can a supreme central authority be created out of the welter of conflicting nations and peoples who now inhabit the earth? Who will rule? Who will obey? Even if personnel to staff a supreme authority could be agreed upon, how could they acquire a strong and united will? How could they agree among themselves?

To these questions there is no answer. Voluntary federations which have endured and prospered are few in history, and those few have nearly always been founded under the stimulus of common fear of some outside danger. Moreover, the enormous diversity of political, economic, and moral conditions among men makes inconceivable any universal or near-universal agreement as to the aims and methods, the personnel and policies, of a world government. The disappointing careers of the League of Nations and of the United Nations show how little ready nations are to submit their quarrels to the judgment of their peers. Still less are existing nations ready to raise over themselves a new authority which would be able to coerce them in future.

Yet it is equally absurd to believe that the political organization of the world which happens to exist in our own day is permanent, natural, or incapable of drastic change. Nation-states have not always existed and do not now exist in all parts of the world. To suppose that men's primary loyalties must always attach to nationality is quite as foolish as to suppose that a particular fashion of clothes will endure forever. The last five or six generations have seen a widespread transfer of human loyalty from locality to nationality. Why should the process stop permanently and forever at national boundaries? Indeed, it seems to me that in proportion as the national unit ceases to be capable of serving public and private needs; in proportion as national governments cease to be able to protect themselves and their people from dangers and difficulties both external and internal; in proportion as transnational power organizations become stronger, their activity more pervasive, their policies more important than separate national policies— in proportion as these changes come to pass, it seems altogether likely that men's loyalties will slowly follow along after the shift in real power and begin to attach themselves to growing, larger units of government.

Military and economic considerations alike are acting in our own time to create two such transnational organizations of power, the one centered in the Union of Soviet Socialist Republics, the other in the United States of America. Unless some check comes to their development, there is good reason to suppose that real sovereignty will more and more rest upon these supranational units of government.

Patriotism has followed power more than once in the past. Rome's subjects became Rome's citizens; and there was once a time in European history when national governments and national patriotism were unknown. The oldest nation-states of Europe did not spring fully grown upon the stage of history. On the contrary, they were formed by degrees from a welter of feudal principalities; and it was only after royal administration had gradually extended its tentacles through the existing political fabric, curbing the independent power of barons, bishops, and cities, that sentiments of loyalty to the national unit grew strong enough to become an important political force. Setting out merely to increase their own power, income, and security against the feudality, medieval kings of England, France, and (with differences) Spain accidentally created nations. After the power and effectiveness of these national units came to be demonstrated, both at home and abroad, others both in Europe and outside it, at length set out to imitate the example of the Western nations, seeing in the nation-state a sort of talisman to power and prosperity. Thus it happened that nationalism in the nineteenth and twentieth centuries came to be separated from power and, instead of following after, preceded the establishment of national governments in Germany, Italy, the lesser countries of eastern Europe, and in South America and large parts of Asia as well.

The growth of any future unit of government which will be better able to cope with the problems confronting human society in our time seems sure to follow the medieval rather than the modern example. New molds of government are required and are in fact already developing by a process of piecemeal improvisation. Nearly all men's political loyalties still cling to the familiar national units, as the medieval peasant clung to his village and the townsman to his town; but this need not prevent the further strengthening of transnational units of government. Periodic emergencies can, I think, be counted upon to push the separate national governments of the earth toward new surrenders of power to a larger whole, for that is the path along which both military security and economic prosperity beckon.

The role once played by the kings of France or of England is today being played by the governments of the United States and of the Soviet Union. And just as medieval kings built themselves first a kingdom and then a nation, so it seems probable that the Russian and American governments will find that they have set out on a path leading first to a world government and then to a world community.

Certainly the American government and the American people have no such conscious intention. The overwhelming majority of my countrymen will recoil from the thought of abandoning the tried and true frontiers of

Americanism in favor of some larger whole. Yet, given contemporary technical and military facts, if a people and a government seriously set their hand to the task of trying to assure military security and economic stability for themselves, there can be no stopping point short of world sovereignty; and, should success crown such an effort, there seems every likelihood that over a period of generations (perhaps centuries) a functioning and effective world government would attract the loyalty of most of the peoples of the earth.

2

If indeed humanity has set its feet on the path toward world government, it is obvious that the way will be long and arduous. When one considers the record of the past, so full of bloodshed and violence, and when one surveys the world of the present with its bitter antagonisms and sporadic warfare, it becomes hard—indeed, I should say impossible—to doubt that more bloodshed and war lie ahead. The armaments race between the United States and the Soviet Union does not seem likely to lead to a peaceable conclusion. Of course neither side fully believes that war lies ahead. The Russians officially argue that internal collapse is sure to come sooner or later to the capitalist world, making their victory—or, rather, the victory of communism—a certainty. The American government has expressed the hope that at some time in the future the free world will have gained such indefeasible military preponderance that the Russians and their satellites will be compelled to negotiate a settlement and to accept in good faith the legal and moral principles set forth in the United

Nations Charter as a guide to their subsequent international policy.

In the light of history neither of these versions of the future seems convincing. The adaptability of capitalist society has notoriously disappointed Communist hopes in the past and is likely to do so in future. It is supremely ironical but nonetheless true that the arms race, resulting from the Soviet threat, helps to insulate the leading non-Communist economies from the alternation of boom and slump which was once the main reliance of Communist hopes. Indeed, the very fact that the Soviet state stands waiting eagerly for internal disruption, forwarding it wherever possible, creates important obstacles to the fulfilment of Marxist prophecy. In proportion as revolutionary agents become obedient tools of Moscow, they become traitors to their own kind; and, in proportion as local independence among revolutionary organizations is maintained against the pressure of Moscow, then seeds of postrevolutionary disruption are present, as Tito's career evidences.

Equally, the American plan of bringing the Russians to their senses by confronting them with overwhelming power seems unlikely to work in practice. No one has publicly set forth terms of settlement which would satisfy the free world; and, indeed, what could satisfy the American and western European nations short of a breakup of the transnational power organization which the Russians have so energetically constructed during the past ten years? But governments are always loath to abandon power and are still more loath to put themselves at the mercy of some other government or power. Men and governments have repeatedly proved themselves willing to fight, even against apparently overwhelming odds, rather than submit to such a fate.

This is not to say that temporary and partial diplomatic adjustments may not be made from time to time. But mutual suspicion and fear, mutual distrust of the good faith of the other party to the negotiation—indeed, the whole divergence of attitude and tradition which separates the Russians from the Western powers—make such diplomatic adjustment difficult. Except for a still precarious truce in Korea, negotiation has achieved little up to the present (1953). But even should diplomacy prove more successful than it has in the recent past, it would at best be palliative. Negotiation and compromise might postpone head-on conflict and a third world war, perhaps for a number of decades, but diplomacy will never be able to remove the basic conflict, the basic fear, which drives each of the two great transnational organizations of power to improve its own preparation for war in the expectation of attack sooner or later.

The best that diplomacy might do would be to prolong the cold war we now endure, to limit future armed clashes to local wars such as that recently suspended in Korea, and to adjust some of the points of international friction until such time as new power centers might arise and transform our bipolar world into something more like the old European balance of power.

But the world has become very small. There hardly seems room on the face of the earth for new powers to arise which would be capable of challenging on equal terms the power presently commanded by the United States and its allies, on the one hand, and by the U.S.S.R. and its satellites and allies, on the other. Vast area, vast population, vast resources, complex industry, skilled technicians, and a numerous, well-equipped and well-trained armed establishment all would be requisite before a new world power could rise to transform the political balance of the world. Only China and India seem to have the possibility; and, if the cold war between the Communist and free worlds were prolonged for at least half a century, it is conceivable that one or both of these Asian nations might rise to the status of a world power, independent of and roughly equal to either of the two power groups which now exist. Any shorter time hardly seems adequate to allow the profound social and technical transformations which would be necessary before such a shift in the balance of power could come to pass.

If one imagines a world in which four great powers found elbow room—the U.S.A., the U.S.S.R., China, and India—one would have a political pattern not unlike that which used to exist in Europe when a number of great powers checked one another's aggrandizement partly by diplomacy and partly by resort to limited, local wars.

Such a picture strains credulity. For one thing, the community of attitude which bounds the nations and empires of Europe into a single civilization would be lacking between our hypothetical great powers of the future. The rules of the old European diplomatic and military game were irrevocably broken in World War I by the European nations themselves through their invention of total war mobilization. With ideological and racial fires to fan future hostility, it is impossible to believe that the limited warfare and balance-of-power diplomacy of the past can be resuscitated.

Second, the rise of a new great power within the European ambit never took place without a bout of general war. Until proved against them on the field of battle, old powers were never willing to admit the claims of newcomers to territory and influence. It seems therefore improbable that China or India could rise to the position we have imagined without engaging in an all-out war with one or other or both of the existing great powers. Diplomacy, no matter how skilful, could hardly localize such a struggle. Cold war would in such circumstances almost certainly become World War III. The incipient development of a new intercontinental balance of power would be plunged into the hot crucible of a general war—the crucible which in the past forty years has eliminated all but two great powers from the face of the earth and which in the future seems far more likely to eliminate other great powers or would-be great powers than to signalize the arrival of new ones.

Third, there are such serious internal obstacles to the successful social and political reorganization of both India and China that one may doubt whether either of these peoples will be able to thrust their way forward and become the military equals of the two existing great-power systems. Neither China nor India now has a very extensive industry; and, while Russia's example shows how rapidly new industry can, under certain circumstances, be created, I have already argued that the circumstances which confront India and China are not so favorable as Russia's were thirty-five years ago. Population pressure is greater, and agrarian poverty is deeper. Moreover, a people which has been steeped in a completely different civilized tradition is likely to be more resistant to the sort of superficial, technological Westernization which would be needful. Russia's native non-Western civilization was, after all, both weaker and intrinsically closer to the civilization of the West than is the civilization of either India or China. Social and psychological obstacles to industrialization and militarization, Western style, were, one may at least suspect, correspondingly weaker in Russia than they are today in the Far East.[1]

In effect, then, two possible lines of future political evolution seem to offer themselves. Either diplomats and governments will be able to adjust and cushion disputes between the two existing major power groups for a period of two or three generations until new and independent powers arise or they will fail to do so. If they fail, we must expect World War III to burst upon the nations and peoples of

1. Japan's case might seem to argue against this view. But, through the centuries, Japan has aped the civilization of China, and it was therefore simply a tour de force, though a remarkable one, for Japanese leaders to transfer their imitation from China to the West. Japanese native civilization was not thoroughly Japanese, any more than Russian civilization, derived largely from Byzantium, was thoroughly and completely Russian. Indeed, Russia's historical relationship to classical and Western civilization seems strictly comparable to Japan's relationship to the civilization of China. Both were offshoots of a major stem; and, in general, the leaders of both Russian and Japanese society felt a sense of inferiority vis-à-vis the main stem from which they had sprung. Both peoples, therefore, could find it in their hearts to reject their only half-satisfactory pasts by accepting Western patterns of industrialism with enthusiasm. No comparable enthusiasm can be expected of the Chinese or Indian peoples, whose attachment to past traditions is all the greater because their respective pasts are so completely their own.

the earth. If they succeed, humanity's agony will, I think, simply be prolonged, perhaps for as much as a century, until further wars lead to the elimination of all but one contender for the political and military leadership of the world.

Contemporary world politics is like a choppy sea in which two opposing currents meet. On the one hand, there is the current in human affairs which impels men and governments to unite into larger and larger military-political associations, seeking thereby an as yet illusory security and stability. This current has set in strongly in the Western and especially in the European parts of the earth. Opposing it is the current which impels certain peoples and governments to withdraw inside existing political frontiers in the hope of strengthening themselves by industrial and military development until such time as they can successfully claim true sovereignty and full equality with the old established nations of the earth. This is the current that dominates Asia and the Middle East.

But we must expect any such withdrawal to be temporary. If, after a few decades of seclusion, a successful reorganization of society should be achieved, the new power would be used to win political, military, and economic influence in neighboring countries, just as today the United States and the Soviet Union are using their new-found power to surround themselves with allied and dependent states. If nothing should happen to interrupt the process, India's current withdrawal from the major conflicts of the world might prove to be the first phase of a parallel evolution. In China's case it seems that, for the time being at least, the impulse toward withdrawal has been canceled by premature involvement in the struggle between the already established great powers.

China's case is, indeed, instructive. Even if they wanted to (and it is not sure that they do), the Chinese Communists have not been able to dissociate themselves from active participation in the Russian-American struggle for "security" against one another. China's intervention in Korea must have had the effect of increasing China's dependence upon the U.S.S.R. for military supplies, economic succor, and diplomatic support. Instead of setting out to build a separate base of power within China, the Communists were caught up in a greater struggle before they had time to take breath; and, the more deeply they immersed themselves in Korea, the more tightly they were bound to the Russian orbit.

India, in a more secure geographical position behind the Himalayas, is not so immediately caught up in the world contest between Russia and America; yet it will surely be difficult for the Indian government to keep aloof and neutral indefinitely. The existence of a formidable Communist party in Indian domestic politics and the dependence of the Indian economy upon imports, not only of machinery but also of food, make that nation vulnerable to pressures which are or may in the future be exerted by the two existing great powers.

Thus the recent course of world events points in the same direction as did our general consideration of the obstacles to the peaceable rise of independent great powers in Asia. Unfortunately for the aspirations of Asian nationalists, the world is no longer what it was even a generation back. When the United States and Russia rose to their present world positions, they did so in what was, by comparison with contemporary conditions, a power vacuum. The United States was particularly fortunate. Between 1865 and 1898, Americans were able virtually to avoid having any sort of foreign policy. No danger threatened from any outside quarter. The breathing space between a bitter civil war and future international wars was used to build up a great industrial base for world power. The Soviet Union was not so free to turn attention inward, nor did its respite, such as it was, last so long. Nevertheless, between 1922 and 1939 the Russians were not actively molested from outside. Precisely because of the ideological antipathy existing between themselves and the other nations of the earth, the Communists were left strictly to themselves and were able to concentrate effort on building an industry and a military establishment which has now become the basis for the world power of the Soviet Union.

No comparable respite for internal development seems likely to be available today. The struggle for power and influence in Asia between the Communist and the free worlds is both conscious and acute. As a result, both the Indians and the Chinese face a dilemma. They cannot assert full independence and equality without a stronger industrial and military base than either nation now possesses, and at the same time they are unable to create such a base except through close association with one or the other grouping of the already established great powers. Whatever growth of industrial and military strength may lie immediately ahead for the two Asian nations is therefore likely to be woven into the existing bipolar power pattern of the world. Only a great wrench, which would almost surely precipitate a third world war, would permit either India or China to launch itself as a full-blown third (or fourth) force, belonging to no camp but its own.

Nevertheless, one should not jump to conclusions. The world may perhaps be destined to pass through a period of intercontinental balance of power; but I believe the greater probability lies on the other side. Instead of seeing the rise of new Asian world powers, humanity is more likely to witness the elimination of one of the two existing contenders for world leadership—as a result of World War III.

Occasions for conflict between the Communist and free worlds are certainly not far to seek. Yet each side dreads all-out war, and neither side is today looking for provocation and excuses to attack. Yet, however great the dread of war may be, it seems quite possible that some act or decision (perhaps an act or decision made by a minor nation) will sooner or later place the two great powers in a position from which neither the one nor the other will be willing to back down. World War I broke out in just such a fashion, and World War III might start similarly. Suppose, for example, a revolution in one of the Soviet satellites should occur; what would happen then? Or, conversely, suppose that one of the nations within the circle of the free world suffered Communist revolution and appealed for Russian assistance? A series of incidents such as these might harden the hearts of the opposing peoples and governments and lead them to resolve against any further retreat, any further compromise, any further undermining of their security. And, having so resolved, they might, when the next crisis broke, act as rigidly as did the Austrian,

Russian, German, and French governments in the fateful days of June and July, 1914.

In 1914, to be sure, no one appreciated the full horrors and dangers of mechanized war. Perhaps now, after two world wars, incidents alone will not suffice to bring on a third. But there is always the possibility that some major shift in the balance of power—Communist revolution throughout the Middle East or in India, for example, or anti-Communist revolt in eastern Germany—might seem such a vital threat to the security of one side and might offer such advantages to the other that it could not or would not hold back from war.

Further, there can be no guaranty that the mood of peoples and governments will not shift. A sense of desperation —that anything is better than an indefinite continuance of tension—may gain ground on either or both sides of the iron curtain. Again, some new weapon of war might convince the leaders of one side or the other that victory at relatively small cost lay within their grasp. Finally, there is the possibility of some internal upheaval within one or the other camp. This might take many forms. A new economic depression or some rupture between the United States and its present allies might offer Russia a chance too good to miss; palace feuds within the Kremlin arising between groups of ambitious men who wished to seize dictatorial power might provide occasion for the secession of some of Russia's satellites or might even provoke some new revolution in Russia itself. Any such sudden jar to the precariously balanced forces of the cold war might lead to World War III.

Even short of overt upheavals such as these, it must be

recognized that one of the oldest of all political maneuvers is to turn attention from difficulties at home by picking a quarrel with an outsider. Since there is no prospect that domestic difficulties will disappear within either the Communist or the free worlds, such a diversion into foreign adventure will be a standing temptation for both sides. Another factor which might help to provoke war is the thirst for fame—the desire to make a mark on history—which, however old-fashioned it may seem, may still become a serious motive with the individual men on either side upon whom an ultimate decision between peace or war may some day devolve.

If, then, possible occasions for the outbreak of war are so numerous while the basis for diplomatic adjustment and compromise is so tenuous, one is compelled to conclude that world war will probably break out once again and engulf the leading states and peoples of the world. It seems to me likely to come fairly soon—within the next thirty years or so.

Perhaps the reader may object that all this hypothetical argument simply overlooks the best and only true hope of mankind, namely, that the governments and peoples of the world will find it possible by slow degrees to build up an enforcible body of international law under the aegis of the United Nations. After all, war is extremely unpopular with those who must wage it—the common people of every land. Is it, then, too much to hope that the pressure of public opinion and the efforts of governments may prevent a third world war and gradually knit all the nations together until international disputes can be settled by legal process?

Hopes such as this have been fairly widespread among Americans in recent decades; and sentiments such as these certainly have had positive effects, as when they helped to support the decision of our government to take action in Korea in 1950. Yet it seems to me that most of the men who advocate a system of world law under the United Nations have not truly thought through what it is they desire for the future and have not taken adequate account of the obstacles that stand in the way of a peaceable and gradual solution of the present political ills of the world. In particular, the question of how Americans (or any other people) could be persuaded by mere argument to allow foreigners to have some say in their domestic affairs and agree to give foreigners a veto power over acts of their national government has seldom been seriously faced by international idealists.

Actually, what many Americans expect or assume when they speak of a future world of international law is a world in which American domestic institutions would be left almost intact, while the other peoples of the world rallied round the standard of morality and legality so stalwartly exemplified by the international conduct of the American government.[2] But to assume that all the peoples of the earth

2. The usual American image of satisfactory international co-operation is, perhaps, drawn largely from the experience of the United States in its relations with other nations of the New World. Many Americans were and are tempted to believe our good relations with Latin America and Canada could be duplicated on the world scene, failing to recognize that the effective preponderance of United States power in the New World was what made the "Good Neighbor" system maintain peace as well as it actually has. Only if one nation's power becomes as overwhelming throughout the world as the power of the United States is now in the New World would a similar "Good Neighbor" policy be likely to eliminate international war.

will swarm round seeking conversion to the gospel of Americanism is surely ridiculous. Only when the presumed basis for international legality is left unexpressed does such a program for the future appear in the least plausible.

As a matter of fact, the attitude of mind I have imputed to the majority of those who argue for the gradual growth of a system of international law within the existing United Nations framework is exactly the frame of mind that permits and encourages international wars. Honest, dutiful, just, convinced of the necessity of retaining one's own national institutions, and persuaded of the desirability of inducing others to imitate them: these are exactly the people who can fight a war with good conscience. To such minds quarrels with a foreign nation promptly become struggles for sacred principle.

Indeed, it seems to me that we face a most trying dilemma. The more tightly knit a given society, the more difficult it is to avoid hostilities with outsiders; the more emphatically individual persons believe that the way they are accustomed to doing things is the only right way of doing them, the more certain they are to quarrel with foreigners. Yet a tight-knit society whose ways seem naturally and certainly right to its members is the sort of society in which men can most easily feel psychologically at home. Such a society is the sort in which nearly all the generations of mankind lived out their lives and to which, I at least believe, our inherent psychological nature inclines us. Only by sacrificing some of the close-fiberedness of society, only by permitting the ingress of foreigners with their odd and undependable moral habits, only by modifying ancestral mores, and only by tolerating alien interference in one's own domestic affairs, can the danger of war be overcome. This is a heavy price to pay; yet, as I have already argued, it seems to me preferable to the alternative of recurrent and increasingly violent paroxysms of international war.

What, then, of the idealistic hope for gradual and peaceable evolution of enforcible international law? Can men be persuaded to abandon the good old ways and to regard the most outrageous acts of foreigners as no more outrageous than their own conduct? I do not think so. History shows how persistent and widespread has been the resort to violence between independent organized groupings of men. Is there any reason to think that men in the twentieth century have changed in such a way as to slough off the heritage of war? History shows too, I believe, that major political changes have not been made without the use of force. Is there any reason to think that men now are so different from their ancestors as to make it possible for them to erect an international government peaceably?

It is sometimes urged that, because modern weapons are so destructive, the very terror they inspire will deter and in the end prevent new war. Again, an appeal to the past shows that new and more terrible weapons have not prevented recurrent warfare. Gunpowder once seemed as monstrous as atom bombs seem now; but is there any reason to think that men will refrain from using the new weapon because the explosive force of atom bombs is greater than that of gunpowder?

As a matter of fact, it has become fashionable to exaggerate the consequences of another world war, even of a war waged with atomic weapons. Horror, destruction, death in many forms would certainly come; and it is likely (but not certain) that they would come on a scale greater than ever before. War would not, however, be at all likely to end civilization. It would change most of the human societies of the earth—some of them radically. It would also be likely to change nearly all, of them for the worse, sacrificing humane pursuits and individuality in favor of the military virtues and social conformity. But human society is very tough, and one may confidently expect that even after another world war the major outlines of most of the societies that now inhabit the globe would still be recognizable, would still resemble their present selves in most respects. Thus should western Europe and the United States ever fall under Communist control as a result of defeat in war, it may safely be predicted that the western European and American examples of Communist society would not be identical with the Russian; and all the efforts of the Russians could not make them so. Similarly, a victory for the free world would not transform the Russians or the Chinese or the peoples of eastern Europe into parliamentary democrats, however much the victorious nations wished to make them over on such lines.

What makes war so terrible in our time is of course the power which machinery and the products of machinery impart to the military arm. Hundreds of thousands of lives can be snuffed out in a moment by an atom bomb. Whole cities may be laid waste by attack from a base halfway round the world. Millions of men can be armed to slaughter one another, and even so-called civilians can be mobilized to work at tasks that strengthen their nation for war. But the harnessing of machinery to war and the elaboration of administrative methods for mobilizing men and resources for battle has inherent limitations which are of the highest importance. Modern war has become an exceedingly complicated matter, involving a relatively delicate and precise co-ordination between the activities of millions—indeed, hundreds of millions—of men. Should that co-ordination fail, the whole effort collapses. Guns without ammunition become useless hardware; airplanes without fuel become unwieldy pieces of inert metal; soldiers without food become helpless human beings. Only the regular operation of a vast and exceedingly complex service of supply—and, behind that, of production—can keep war going.

The very complexity of the supply problem makes modern war machines fragile and delicate in comparison with the simpler, less powerful, and less vulnerable armies that trod the earth in former times. It follows that wars of total destruction cannot be fought under modern conditions. Long before a population has been entirely wiped out, long before most of a country's factories and mines have been destroyed, even long before the last round of ammunition or gallon of gasoline has been consumed—in short, long before destruction has become total, the co-ordination which is indispensable for the prosecution of war is certain to break down. Transport is the most vulnerable link in any war economy. If things cannot be delivered to the right place at the right time in more or less the right quantity—and this all down the line from raw material to finished munitions of war—then the fighting capacity of the armed forces evaporates within a very short time. As supplies dry up, the will to fight can be depended on to crumble *pari passu,* if, indeed, morale does not collapse before logistical breakdown has fully done its work.

The ancient Spartans could fight quite literally to the last man. Once a Spartan hoplite had been equipped with sword, shield, and a bag of barley, he was complete, self-sufficient, independent of rear services of supply for as long as his barley held out. And food could sometimes be found locally, whether by pillage or purchase. A detachment of a modern army can of course duplicate the feat of Leonidas and his men; but no large modern army can hope to do so. Supplies would be sure to give out before the last life was expended, and, without supplies, what use is there in defying tanks, airplanes, or even rifles with bare hands?

These obvious facts—and they are facts—go far to explain the manner in which both the first and the second World Wars came to an end. In neither war was the German population wiped out; in neither war were German factories entirely (or even mostly) destroyed; in neither war was the fabric of German society so broken that a rapid recovery could not take place. Japan's case in World War II was even more striking. Before Japanese society, government, or economy had begun to dissolve, further resistance became so obviously suicidal that surrender seemed the better course. One may expect a third world war to end similarly, when the sinews of war begin to fail one of the major combatants as a result of the breakdown of a co-ordinated flow of supplies to the fighting fronts but before total destruction or anything close to it has occurred.

While it is possible to take some comfort from these considerations, one must also recognize that total destruction, or something very near to it, may come to the peoples who happen to inhabit the battlegrounds of a future world war. With airplanes, rockets, and who knows what other long-range weapons, any future battleground is likely to extend through zones perhaps hundreds of miles deep. It will not be the endurance of the peoples who live in these zones that will determine the length of the fighting. Hostile armies, depending upon supplies brought from afar, might easily grind the peoples living in the area of their battleground into dust before one or the other gained a decisive advantage.

This situation is not new. The inhabitants of some of the small islands of the Pacific must have come near extinction in World War II. In Europe the fate of the civilian population even in battle zones was not so desperate. Flight or burrowing provided refuge for the great majority, whatever the discomforts. Yet in Europe, too, some districts and towns were almost completely destroyed and temporarily depopulated. Survival in a battle zone will not likely be so easy again. Flight will be harder as battle zones widen, perhaps to engulf whole countries; and burrowing will not be adequate protection against more powerful and indiscriminate weapons. It is, indeed, conceivable that all of western and central Europe might become one vast battle zone and that in a third world war European society and civilization as we know it might suffer irreparable destruction. This is what all Europeans fear.

But there can be no certainty in the matter. The occasion and course of a future war are quite unforeseeable. It might happen, for instance, that the opposing armies would each be so well dug in in Europe that neither would feel it practicable to try to attack head-on. Other battlefields could then be found. The Middle East, northern China and Manchuria, or Alaska and western Canada might turn out to be major theaters of war. There is also the possibility that a third world war might prove to be short and sharp. One or the other side might collapse from within under the initial blows; or some new weapon or skilful propaganda might turn the tables before the war was many months old. On the other hand, a war lasting for long years cannot be ruled out, and it is conceivable that the result would be a complete stalemate. This, the worst of all possible outcomes, would make the fighting completely futile and most horribly destructive.

Fortunately, stalemate seems so unlikely as to verge on the impossible. The very intensity with which modern war is fought makes it difficult, perhaps impossible, to maintain the effort at full pitch for more than a few years. In four or five years vast movements of men and materials might take place, tremendous campaigns might be fought, and the full military strength of the contestants could be brought to bear. In such a struggle even a small margin of superiority might make the difference between defeat and victory; even a small margin of tenacity, daring, or plain luck might abruptly convert a seeming stalemate into sudden victory, which would be as complete as those of the first two World Wars.

This is but another way of saying what has been said already. Modern war machines, for all their power, are fragile. When once they begin to collapse, collapse is sure to be both sudden and complete, making the last stages of the war a victory parade for the winning side. When endurance, courage, and faith are strained to the breaking point, a tiny advantage may suffice to tip the scales. A small success in the field, a panic among troops or among the chiefs of government, internal *coup d'état,* the defection of allies, or the intervention of some fresh power which had been neutral in the war's first stages—any of these things might be just enough to turn stalemate into a decision.

The bitterness of the ideological conflict between the Communist and free worlds make a diplomatic compromise or negotiated peace unlikely, should battle once be joined. One can imagine an interlude should the Russians manage to overrun all Eurasia and Africa and then find themselves confronted by ocean barriers before they could again come to grips with American forces. Such a situation might even lead to an armistice and peace treaty; but a peace concluded under such circumstances would very likely turn out to be either a prelude to Communist revolution in the United States or else merely a breathing spell while each side gathered strength for a second and final round. On the other hand, should success incline toward the free world, there seems no possible halting point short of Soviet surrender. Such surrender need not be unconditional, but—barring some incredible shortsightedness on the part of the victor—it would be decisive, making any further resumption of the conflict impossible.

There is a cruel irony in the fact that, just because in any general war fought within the next thirty years the major means of battle and the strongest will to victory would come from the Russian and American heartlands, for that very reason these lands could not undergo irreparable physical or social damage from such a war. As soon as one or the other began to suffer seriously from war's destruction, it would be impossible to continue organized battle much longer, and collapse would ensue within a few months. The war would be over at last, quite conceivably leaving Europe and some other parts of the earth in smoking ruins, but most assuredly leaving the homeland of both the principal victor and the principal vanquished state in a condition from which recovery would be possible and, indeed, relatively easy.

Only should the victor decide in cold blood to eliminate all traces of his rival would complete and irreparable destruction come to either of the protagonists in a future war. In 146 B.C. the Romans sowed the ruins of Carthage with salt and formally cursed any man bold enough to think of restoring their dreaded rival; but such a policy in the twentieth century A.D. seems out of the question. Wanton destruction would needlessly deprive the victor of resources he could otherwise use for his own purposes. Despite all the bitterness the Nazis aroused against the German nation, it is instructive to recall that within a few months of victory both the Russians and the Western powers found themselves busy restoring the German economy. Their motives were not primarily humanitarian; rather, their actions were taken because only with a German economy in running order could the costs of reparations and occupation be met from German resources.

3

Let us, then, assume as probable a third world war, leading to the decisive victory of either the Communist or the free world. What shape would such a postwar world be likely to take?

Much would depend on the length and severity of the war itself, and that is something that cannot profitably be surmised. The longer the war, the more difficult the recovery and the less likely that the victorious alliance would have any margin to spare for the relief of devastated and conquered countries. Without large-scale relief, famine and epidemic would be likely to stalk the world for some time after the fighting ended, and they might even invade the homeland of the victors. But, for all that, revolution or internal paralysis among the victors is not to be expected. The psychological *élan* of victory is great in itself, and the victorious governments could hold out hope of better times to come should their own peoples show signs of restlessness in the immediate postwar period. On the other hand, revolution among the vanquished would be a certainty; and there is a possibility that civil or guerrilla war might prevail for some years to devastate and debilitate the conquered nations still further.

The immediate terms of peace might very well follow the pattern set by the victors in the first and second World Wars: disarmament of the vanquished, reparations, punishment of "war criminals," occupation of at least a part of the enemy country by the victors' forces. Quarrels among the members of the victorious alliance should be expected. Victorious allies have nearly always quarreled in the hour of victory, and there seems no reason why they should not do so again. But after a war fought between the Communist and the free worlds, there would be far less scope for such quarrels than there has been in the past. At any rate, if the war is fought within the next thirty years, it seems very probable that either the Soviet Union or the United States will enjoy an unchallengeable preponderance among the members of the victorious alliance. Quarrels could therefore scarcely lead to the division of the world once again into two rival and approximately equal armed camps. Unless the dominant power among the victors proved strangely maladroit or savagely tyrannous, one might therefore expect not a new cold war but a new world government to emerge from the ruins of the battlefield.

The most critical immediate postwar problem would be to decide how armed force should be distributed among the nations. On this would depend the possibility of international peace; and upon the establishment of such a peace would depend the possibility of some mitigation of the economic, racial, and moral problems which now so bedevil mankind. Observations on each of these aspects of a possible post–World War III settlement follow.

4

The Problem of Military Security.—Only if some single and reliably united will could command overwhelming military force would the likelihood of further wars disappear. This is even now to the general interest of all mankind and after a third world war would be far more obviously so. Only if the dominant nation among the victors so arranged matters that its own government commanded overwhelming military force would its newly won position be secure. Thus the selfish, nationalistic sentiments of the principal victor and the interests of the overwhelming majority of mankind would coincide. Such a coincidence would vastly increase the likelihood that an effective monopoly of at least the capital weapons of war would in actual fact be established. A system of inspection to guard against clandestine rearmament would also be essential.

There are a variety of methods by which a concentration of military power might occur. The principal victor might retain a separate national armament while requiring a partial disarmament of other nations. On the other hand, direction of a world army might be intrusted to something like the United Nations or to a revived Comintern, but under conditions and with stipulations which would in fact assure that the dominant power among the victors could effectively control the new international force. Still a third possibility would be a combination of both methods, whereby an international force and a single great national force remained in existence, with both under the ultimate control of the same government.

The question of how armaments should be distributed and controlled would be one which might easily provide the mainspring of quarrel among erstwhile allies. No government would welcome a situation in which it would become helpless to oppose intervention from outside. But the general advantage to be expected from the concentration of supreme armed force in a single hand would be obvious to everyone. Such concentration would end international war as we know it today and banish the terrible specter of yet further wars. Particularly if the dominant power were to show tact enough to put the armed force under at least nominal international control, widespread world opinion might well support the concentration of predominant military strength into a single hand. Arrangements for consultation with representatives of allied governments could safely be made. Contingents from the armed forces of other nations would not destroy the effectiveness of the international armed establishment and might rather improve its effectiveness.

It is altogether likely that the major outlines of any postwar military settlement would in reality be worked out during or even before the war. One can safely assume that both the free world and the Communist world would fight under a unified command—a command in which Americans and Russians would, respectively, predominate. It follows that a prolongation of the wartime system of military administration into peace, and its adjustment to whatever form of international political organization might emerge, would suffice to maintain effective unitary control of an overwhelmingly powerful armed force. When the members of the victorious alliance began to discuss the future military establishments of the world, they would not begin with a *tabula rasa*. Their task would be easier. They would have only to adjust what lay already at hand; and a continuance of the wartime concentration of military power under a single supreme command might present an aspect not of usurpation but of a willingness and capacity to bear the cost of policing the world.

This line of argument is no longer purely theoretical. Both in Korea and in Europe, an international organization of armed force has been and continues to be sustained and, in essentials, controlled by the government of the United States. Russian influence over the armed forces of its European satellites is certainly as strong and probably stronger.

In each case the embryo from which a future unified control of a world-wide international armed force might grow can clearly be discerned.

Concentration of overwhelming, unchallengeable military power in a reliably united supreme command would provide the indispensable prerequisite for a gradual development of effective international law and of administrative agencies to apply it to disputes as they arose. This is another way of saying that the concentration of an unchallengeable force in a reliably united single command would open the path for an international government. Such a government would function because of the *de facto* predominance of a single nation (or, perhaps, of a closely associated group of nations); but it might nonetheless register the wishes and complaints of others. At the least, all the peoples and states of the earth would have their day in court; at the best, all would have a genuine if limited part in determining the governance of the world.

The first task of any government is to keep a modicum of peace within its jurisdiction. Peace has never been absolute; violence has always broken out among men. Indeed, the sort of loose international government which I imagine would probably first emerge after another world war might tolerate a greater degree of violence than a government more strongly founded in public sentiment would do. Violence might indeed run to the level of low-grade local wars, analogous, for example, to the battles fought in Palestine in 1946–48. So long as no vital interest of the dominant power were at stake, it might hesitate to intervene in local quarrels, and, without a firm impulse from the dominant power, international authorities might descend to indecision. But should such local affrays threaten to spread, or should they last very long, then international legal action would surely follow; and in the great majority of cases diplomatic mediation, military blockade, or the mere threat of punitive action by international armed forces would suffice to bring the combatants to some sort of terms.

On a lower level, guerrilla actions, riots, and sporadic mob violence would assuredly continue to plague the nations of the earth wherever social strains and antagonisms became acute. All the states of the world would continue to require a modest armed establishment to safeguard the public peace.

But survival of this sort of violence, and of national armed forces to cope with it, would not detract from the central fact that wars as we know now them would no longer be possible. Men would be freed from the burden of armaments races and from the fear of further cataclysmic war. Systematic preparation for war would no longer be a constant pre-occupation of the various governments of the world, and the peoples of the earth would be free to devote their energies to peaceable pursuits.

The greatest danger to perpetual peace would come from within the ranks of the international army itself. There are three possible situations that might lead to a renewal of large-scale war: personally ambitious generals; development of a military *esprit de corps* in opposition to civilian society and government; or, more serious, recrudescence of racial and cultural antipathies within the ranks of an international force.

Under certain circumstances it is conceivable that the

ambitions and rivalries of individual generals might provoke efforts to subvert established rulers and governments. How serious the danger from this sort of *coup d'état* might be would largely depend on the nature of the government of the dominant power and upon the nature of the international government it supported. The more dictatorial the structure of such governments, the more likely would military *coups d'état* become. A general might easily fancy himself in a dictator's chair and see no path to such a post save through violence. Moreover, public discontent would have more chance to smolder under a dictatorial regime than under a democratic one and might provide an ambitious general with widespread support for his venture. If, on the other hand, a future world government incorporated into itself real and workable democratic elements, and if the government of the dominant power took a democratic form and won the support of a majority of its own citizens, then the danger of military *coup d'état* would not be great. The soldiers would not easily allow themselves to be led against the established authorities, the generals would have less incentive to attempt it, and the public at large would not be likely to support such usurpation if it were attempted.

A second possible cause for civil war would be the development of a psychological gap between soldiers and civilians. The surest way to create such a gap would be for the citizens of the dominant power to turn away from military service, preferring a more comfortable life. In such an event, one might expect upheavals to occur sooner or later within the ranks of the international army. Foreign mercenaries can never be entirely reliable servants, especially should they be recruited, as would almost surely be the case, among poverty-stricken peoples, who would have no great reason to feel that things as they were should always be. Indeed, possession of and exercise in the use of arms is a ball and chain inseparably attached to rulership. A dominant people that neglects the military virtues and way of life entirely will not long hold what its ancestors won; and this, I believe, will be as true in the future as it has been in the past.

Unless a substantial proportion of the rank and file of the future army of the world can feel themselves flesh of one flesh with civilians who, in their turn, voluntarily support the system of national and world government which may evolve, then military revolts become probable. This means that a wise government will recruit soldiers mainly, perhaps exclusively, from peoples whose loyalty to the new order of things can be depended upon. It means also that a purely or predominantly professional force—a force whose members might easily come to feel themselves separate from mere civilians, with interests and grievances peculiar to themselves—would be riskier than a force recruited largely from civilians who expect in a short time to return to civilian pursuits. A professional force might well be more efficient technically; it might also be less amenable to civilian control and, having the means, might develop the will to seize political power itself.

It is clear that the more exclusive and tyrannous the dominant power, the greater its self-inflicted penalty would become. An out-and-out tyrant, holding unwilling peoples in check, must do so by force of arms; and the arms must be wielded by petty tyrants bound to the service of the greater by a common fear and distrust of subject peoples thronging round about. A dominant nation whose policy and conduct won volunatry support among other peoples would require lesser force and would also have a wider field of recruitment for its international army.

But no policy, I think, can within any foreseeable future assure universal support for a new world order such as I have imagined. The defeated will be likely to remember their former greatness; and, more stubborn than such memories, the varieties of mankind, measured by physical appearance and cultural condition, will guarantee a constant friction between the dominant and the subordinate peoples. This would offer by far the most serious possibility for future wars. Chinese and Indians, for example, could not be expected to feel enthusiasm for a world led by either the United States or by the Soviet Union; and, if these peoples were recruited into a future international army in numbers proportionate to their share of the world's population, one could only expect that Asian discontent with the situation emerging from a third world war would in the fulness of time find some form of military expression.

Yet even should defects in the wisdom and moral character of the dominant power create the conditions for recurrent bouts of civil war, the resultant damage to human society would not equal what is today wreaked by recurrent international war. Preparation for civil war within the structure of an international government could not be prolonged and public. It would have to be secret and, necessarily, sketchy. Hostile fragments of an international force would have to battle each other, at least initially, with means already at hand. This in itself would drastically re-

duce the scale of hostilities. Moreover, civil war, even between races, would scarcely command the deep and settled
loyalties which national states can now command, if only
because the background of childhood indoctrination and
the apparatus of partisan propaganda could not be created
in a twinkling. Unless the dominant power had conducted
itself in a tyrannous fashion, the predominant feeling
among civilians the world around would probably be one
of distress if civil war did break out. Their greatest desire
would be to see the struggle quickly ended. Therefore, before separate parts of the earth could be mobilized for war
in the thoroughgoing fashion so familiar today, it would
seem likely that world-wide sentiment would swing behind whichever side seemed to be winning, and the psychological basis for total mobilization of men and resources
would be denied the weaker or less well-situated side.

In other words, civil war would probably become a
struggle between rival parts of a single standing army. The
sort of limited war which vanished from Europe with the
French Revolution would thus be restored; and the peoples of the earth might become willing once again to accept more or less passively the arbitrament of chance and
generalship as worked out among professional soldiers, instead of, as now, dedicating themselves personally and in-
tensely to the success of one or other side.

The reader may feel that such a picture of the future
military structure of the world is ridiculous. When tides of
nationalism are so evidently rising in most of the non-
European world, it may seem unmitigated folly to look
forward to a time when national sentiment might sink into
military ineffectiveness. Yet the wider sweep of history cer-

tainly supports the view that nationalism is not a permanent and inevitable frame of mind among men. History may also be read to support the view, advanced above, that loyalty is likely to follow after and attach itself to practical power. At the very least, those peoples who could not escape feeling that the new world order was essentially alien, imposed upon them from outside, would easily detect the advantages of peace. They might, like the Greek and oriental subjects of Rome, prefer an alien peace to the old chaos.

A wise international government would not need to repress all manifestations of national feeling. It might even, as the Soviet Union has sometimes done, encourage peoples to treasure their peculiar cultural inheritance, while nipping military manifestations of national sentiment in the bud.

In actual fact, the contemporary identification between language, culture, and martial glory is not old. It took modern form only with the French Revolution and has won firm foothold outside western Europe mainly in the twentieth century. Appropriate changes in military administration might therefore make it possible to dissociate the military from the other elements of contemporary nationalism. Indeed, I believe this might turn out to be much easier than at first appears, since the suicidal implications of rival national militarisms have already become painfully clear to all the world.

Before leaving this question, it is proper to point out that the establishment of a supreme world-wide military and political authority would involve losses as well as gains. Whatever transfer of human loyalty from national to international organs of government might eventually prove possible would not change the fact that self-identification with a world-wide whole would necessarily be weaker than are the bonds of nationalism today. Individuals would quite correctly feel that they were by themselves almost wholly powerless to affect the march of events or to modify the policy of an international government. Politics would probably become more than ever a spectator sport, the special province of professional manipulators of mass opinion and feeling and of administrative and technical experts.

Such changes cannot seem desirable to anyone attached to the local, more pliable, more closely knit national state. Yet it is worth remembering that the establishment of national government involved an identical loss. Human attachment to and participation in the affairs of city-states and village communities were much stronger and more intense than anything that could ever be realized within a national unit. But between the twelfth and the nineteenth centuries national governments proved themselves able to do two things local sovereignties could not: they could maintain public peace within the realm and they could permit a fuller economic development by breaking through local customary and legal restrictions. Because these services were valuable, men gradually modified their attachments to localities and in time became nationalists.

Now a future international government might in the twentieth century perform the same services for the peoples of the earth that national governments did in the European past. A world government could maintain a general level of public peace all round the globe much superior to that which now exists, just as the king's peace of the later Middle Ages was much superior to the disorder of feudal war. This has already been argued in sufficient detail. International government might also reasonably be expected to allow (indeed, promote) a fuller economic development among the peoples of the earth. Consideration of this aspect of a post–World War III settlement must concern us next.

5

The Problem of Economic Security.—Establishment of an international authority with the military power and the will to keep the peace would at once relieve mankind from a tremendous economic burden. Relatively small forces would suffice to police a world from which the possibility of large-scale international war had been removed. An international army numbering a few hundred thousand should suffice to meet any foreseeable effort to defy the will of an international government, supported and controlled in the fashion imagined above. Moreover, there would be no need to keep on improving and producing new weapons. Once an international armed force had been equipped with a quota of highly lethal weapons while all other armed forces were deprived of access to them, there would be no reason to devote energy or ingenuity to making such weapons even more powerful. Existing weapons would assure superiority over any potential opponent, and that is all any military man can ask.

Hence the manpower and resources now employed to equip and re-equip armies, navies, and air forces around the world would nearly all be freed for more rewarding economic pursuits; and most of the manpower now under arms would similarly become available for work in factories, shops, farms, or elsewhere.

There would no doubt be difficult problems of readjustment. Economic conversion from war to peace presented its difficulties after the first and second World Wars; and after a third such war it might well happen that a legacy of disorder and destruction would postpone economic reconstruction, at least in some parts of the world, for years after the central struggle had been decided. And, as has been suggested already, some parts of the world, especially Europe, might suffer such damage as to make the restoration of any simulacrum of prewar society quite impossible.

Nevertheless, taking the globe as a whole and focusing attention not on the immediate postwar hardships but on the likely state of things two or three decades after the establishment of a single supreme armed force, it seems probable that men would find ways of increasing the production of both food and industrial goods above anything known today; and, instead of using a substantial proportion of available resources for maintaining and equipping armed men, all, or very nearly all, of the world's product would become available for civil consumption.

This may be unduly optimistic. Obstacles to the full employment of men and resources have proved very stubborn in the past and are sure to continue formidable. Russian methods of centralized planning and governmental control of economic activity have not so far had to adjust to the whims and tastes of consumers. It is, after all, one thing to calculate tons of iron and coal for steel plants to use, and of steel, copper, and aluminum for the production of tanks and airplanes; and it is quite a different thing to try to assign quantities, qualities, prices, raw materials, labor force, wages, production norms, and all the rest for the production of hundreds of thousands of items which men like to consume and which they might have if industrial technique were given free rein. The behemoth of state economic planning on the Russian pattern might prove itself so clumsy an instrument as to be more of a hindrance than a help to consumers' production in a world from which the need to prepare for war had been removed. Moreover, an economy directed toward the satisfaction of consumers' wants would accord ill with an authoritarian political system such as that which today directs Russian economic planning. Workmen and peasants might object to wages and rewards planned for them and might manifest their objection by strikes or by sabotaging production in other ways. They might do so on a scale unparalleled now when the real or fancied danger of military attack from outside lends a degree of plausibility to Russian apologies for their authoritarian methods of controlling their own people. Similarly, the great depression of the 1930's proved how stubborn may be the obstacles to full use of labor and materials within the matrix of American institutions and customs.

These considerations, however, do not deter me from believing that some combination of governmental control with individual and corporate enterprise will be found—a combination which will be able to set men and machines to work on a scale hitherto unknown. Industrial and agricultural techniques are already at hand. No future war can possibly eradicate the knowledge of them, since a large body of skilled industrial engineers and technicians would be required for the conduct of war itself. And to suppose that methods would not be found to bring men and machines together to make goods is to suppose that the economic lessons of the past thirty years have not been learned. Human ingenuity in combination with human needs and desires may, I think, be counted upon to reduce or overcome the social obstacles to full employment.

The outcome of the war would probably make some real differences in world economic affairs. If the Russians should win, they would probably attempt a radical remodeling of economic institutions around the world, intending to make all peoples conform to their own Communist patterns. Such a policy would require a wide use of force and a resort to terrorization and violence. Communist revolutions might, indeed, produce a superficial uniformity in economic institutions everywhere; but it seems sure that underneath such appearance very wide differences would still persist. Habits of mind, attitudes toward work, variations in skill, capital plant, natural resources, and population pressure—all these things would remain to differentiate the various nations and peoples of the earth from one another, making some richer, some poorer, some predominantly industrial, and some predominantly agrarian.

American economic policy would probably be much more piecemeal and more inclined to improvisation. Differences in national ethos and in national economic development would be more likely to find their expression in varying economic institutions. Yet one might expect a strong tendency for other nations to try to imitate and adopt the economic practices of the dominant power; and this, combined with further spead of industrial techniques into hitherto backward areas, might in the course of generations produce a measure of uniformity, at least outwardly. But, again, uniformity would never be complete. Geographical and social differences may be depended on permanently to diversify the economies of the world.

An international government operating under circumstances such as those outlined above would not confine its activities entirely to military and political matters. Various economic functions, analogous to those already undertaken by the United Nations, would be very likely to fall within the scope of international agencies from the start; and I would expect the range of international economic administration to increase steadily, since most of the really important economic problems of the world cannot be adequately handled within merely national boundaries.

At the start, reconstruction of war damage might come under the aegis of an international administration; so might collection of reparations from the vanquished. An effort to gather uniform and reliable economic statistics from all the national governments of the earth would almost surely constitute one of the first undertakings. Such statistics would be an indispensable prerequisite for any systematic attempt to do something about the more serious long-range economic difficulties likely to confront mankind.

Of these, the balance between population and food supply would be one of the most critical and pressing. What the Food and Agricultural Organization of the United Nations is now attempting on a relatively small scale might become a much larger enterprise in future. Of course one cannot foresee how the intervening years and the course of another world war might affect the population problem. It is possible that the war, preceded perhaps by a chronic guerrilla and accompanied by starvation and disease, might so reduce the overdense peasant populations of the earth as to make the whole matter much less urgent than it is today. But such relief would be only temporary unless somehow means were found to expand food production and slow down the multiplication of peasant populations.

The problem does not seem to be intrinsically insoluble. Under some social circumstances the growth of population at least appears to bear a relation to the economic circumstances which confront the parents. This is the case in older industrialized societies today. It is reasonable therefore to suppose that it might prove possible to combine programs of education, migration, agricultural improvement, industrialization, and, last but by no means least, birth control in such a way as to bring population growth and economic productivity into balance. The project would, of course, be vast, and results would come slowly at first. I imagine that something close to a century would be the shortest time in which anything like a stable balance between population and productivity could be achieved in all the major regions of the world. Such a balance would require modification of the most intimate and personal relations of human life among vast populations; and, to effect such changes, the short cuts of force could scarcely be effective.

A second major economic problem that would be likely to come before a future international government would be the regulation of trade between nations. Tariffs, quotas, financial blockages, state trading, and the like would not, I think, disappear; on the contrary, a prolonged period of preparation for war and war itself would probably extend and complicate these devices for controlling the international flow of goods. Moreover, in a post–World War III world, the industrial nations grouped around whichever power might come out on top would have an interest in establishing or maintaining their economic pre-eminence over other parts of the world. Free trade would not be likely to suit their wishes and would therefore be unlikely to eventuate.

Nevertheless, continuance of all-out economic warfare between nations would not be to the interest of the dominant power and its associates. The major motive behind such warfare would, indeed, automatically disappear should the possibility of future war vanish from the earth. National autarky would cease to seem desirable in itself; instead nations might be expected to struggle for more favorable terms of trade, seeking higher prices for their exports while trying at the same time to protect them from competition and to cheapen imports. Obviously national regulations which succeeded in giving one nation's economy such an advantage would be almost certain to hurt some other nation. The whole question of trade regulation might therefore become a matter for complaint and discussion before the supreme political authority of the world. One might expect some effort at adjudication of trade disputes and, perhaps, the gradual development of an enforcible body of international regulations, defining what was and what was not permissible for national governments to do. The Organization for European Economic Co-operation is even now making a start in this direction. In our imagined post–World War III world a similar attempt on a global basis seems probable.

A third major economic problem for a future international organization would be the regulation of industrial expansion, especially expansion into new areas of the earth. A fuller exploitation of the world's natural resources and the discovery and application of improved industrial methods would obviously benefit humanity as a whole in the long run. But any particular new development would in the short run create new competition for old industrial centers and might have the effect of damaging or destroying their prosperity. At the same time, the question of who would supply capital, and on what terms, would be crucial. Whenever capital crossed national frontiers, conflicting economic and political interests between borrower and lender might well become a matter for adjudication by international authorities.

Indeed the pattern, rate, and geographical location of new capital development would have such central significance for the general economic balance of the world that a future international authority would, I think, encourage, even compel, nations and entrepreneurs to present their plans and projects for some sort of official approval, decision, or advice. The International Bank, established during World War II, already performs such a function on a small scale. In a future world settlement, centralized regulation of world capital development might be much extended.

These three problems—food and population, trade, and industrial development—could not be treated in isolation from one another, nor is it likely that any policy could please all parties. Collisions of interest between farmers and industrial producers cannot be removed by any sort of political mediation, nor can the oppositions between lenders and borrowers, employees and managers. It seems quite likely that agrarian unrest and industrial strikes would continue in our hypothetical future to reflect some of these collisions of interest, just as they do now. Only if the dominant power should bring naked military and police power to bear, ruthlessly suppressing strikers and treating rebellious peasants as class enemies, would these manifestations of economic strain fail to appear. And, should such tyranny prevail, I have already suggested that some military manifestation of the represssed discontent might—indeed, probably would—sooner or later break out within the ranks of the international armed forces.

Equable adjudication and mediation between diverse economic interest groups would present serious difficulties. It would require forbearance and understanding of others on the part of the dominant power, whose inclination would certainly be to side with the industrial as against the agrarian interest and with the industrial managers as against the employees. At least to begin with, there would be no clear standard of legal justice, easy to apply to particular cases and acceptable on principle to both parties. The theory that free-market-price mechanism should be allowed to fix terms of trade between industry and agriculture and to determine wage rates and conditions of labor would not suffice, I feel sure. But when political intervention is invoked to fix these highly controversial matters, what standard can be used? What parity can be established? What justice found?

No exercise of human reason is ever likely to provide universally satisfactory answers to such questions. But rule of thumb, making small modifications in favor of one or another economic interest group in accordance with the political pressure it could bring to bear, might, perhaps, serve in future as satisfactorily as it does now in the more advanced industrial states to bring about gradual adjustments while preserving the public peace from serious infraction by economically discontented groups.

6

The Clash of Races and Civilizations.—A world in which the military-political and economic difficulties which today confront mankind had been met in something like the fashion imagined above would still be distracted by the antipathies between races and divergent civilized traditions.

What a post–World War III situation might be would depend very largely upon the course of the war itself and also on the development of relations between nations and civilizations in the decades before war broke out. Should the victorious coalition find in the colored races valuable and much-needed allies, a more nearly equal situation would automatically arise. Should, on the contrary, the war take the form of a white man's struggle, with the Asian nations hostile toward the victor, or distantly neutral, then the ground for profound racial ill-feeling would be laid. Either pattern seems possible; and, regardless of how the major races may align themselves in the present and future struggle, it seems almost certain that antipathy between them and between the different civilizations they sustain will prove more awkward and far more persistent than either military-political or economic problems.

It is obvious that some of the damage which racial and cultural antagonism can wreak among mankind would be canceled at once if the possibility of international war were removed and if a legal-political framework for the adjudication of economic disputes were established. It is possible, too, that a deliberate propaganda praising the brotherhood of man might soften and diminish in the minds, and eventually in the hearts, of men the distrust they feel toward alien colors and cultures. Communist doctrine and the American democratic tradition alike are committed to the proposition that all men are equal; but the practice of Americans leaves much to be desired, and the equality which the Russians in practice afford to men of various races, when it is not bogus altogether, is an equality in slavery. What, if any, changes in the prevailing American and Russian practice might be brought by a third world war must remain an open question.

In general, two divergent lines of development seem possible in a post–World War III world. One conceivable path would lead toward assimilation. The peoples and governments of other races might be won over and embark upon an effort to assimilate their traditions and institutions to those of the dominant power, until, in time, at least the outward differences in civilization would be lessened or removed. Simultaneously, the dominant power and its associates might find things worthy of admiration and imitation among alien peoples. One must expect a one-sidedness in any such assimilation, since in most men's minds the possession of military and political power serves as guaranty that the civilization which has produced such power is *ipso facto* better and more desirable than any other.

It is also possible that intermarriage and interbreeding between men of different race and culture would become far more significant than it is today. If barriers to migration were reduced—as they might be—opportunities for such intermingling would increase. If officials and soldiers of the dominant power were stationed for long periods of time in odd corners of the earth, the same thing would happen, though perhaps not on a scale that would prove demographically significant.

But, when all is said, no foreseeable upheaval seems at all likely to dilute the uniformity of the great demographic reservoirs of the earth—that is, the peasants and farmers. In great cities both cultural and biological intermingling could be expected; in the countryside it would proceed, if at all, at an unimaginably slow rate. Thus elimination of the distinctions of physical appearance which now divide the races of mankind is not likely to occur within any span of time we are accustomed to consider as historical. Changes, perhaps very considerable ones, in the areas occupied by various races might take place as a result of the expansion to new ground of one race of farmers at the expense of another.[3] But such population movements would increase rather than decrease ill-feeling between the races.

3. If political barriers were relaxed, the peoples of India and China might well succeed in making most of the world their own through migration to relatively underpopulated parts of the earth. The history of Manchuria since 1911 shows how rapidly such an expansion may occur. Until some equalization of standards of living and of procreation between the Asian peoples and those of other nations comes to pass, the possibility of Asian demographic conquest of the world will always remain.

This suggests a second major possibility: relations between the races and civilizations might not move toward assimilation but instead toward the establishment of something resembling a caste system. If anything like the sort of political and economic reordering of the world projected above should in fact take place, it would involve the enlargement of zones of mixture where racially and culturally plural societies would take form. But historically it is a fact, I believe, that the participants in a racially and culturally plural society have usually drawn themselves apart into separate communities. Should the dominant power of a post–World War III world maintain a policy of reserving certain favored posts and occupations for its own nationals while refusing to extend citizenship to aliens, then a world ruling caste would arise. Similarly, nations or groups of nations might form into castelike bodies, distinguished from one another partly by occupational specialisms, partly by race and culture, with each such group jealous of its peculiar prerogatives and anxious to guard the integrity of its established racial and cultural character. The major nations and races of the world might thus by degrees transform themselves into castes, geographically intermingled on a scale much greater than now, but nonetheless effectually insulated from racial and cultural contamination by legal or psychological barriers.[4]

A caste society conforms to certain strong human pro-

4. How effective such barriers can be is shown by the history of India. The transformation of Jewry from a nation into a caste—a transformation accomplished in the second century A.D., though begun earlier—is an example of how what I have been imagining might come to pass. The contemporary effort to turn Jewry into a nation once again is a further demonstration of the mutual convertability between caste and nation.

pensities. It combines a physical intermingling, which political and economic relationships may dictate, with cultural isolation; and such cultural isolation provides each individual with a group to which he may cling and with which he may identify himself. It also provides him with aliens to despise, fear, hate. In actual fact, most of the geographically extensive states of the past have exhibited at least traces of such a social system, since they were divided between conquerors and conquered, and often between priest and soldier as well. To refuse to believe that something similar could not happen in the future would be to suppose that human nature has or will somehow change. Racial and cultural antipathies are very deep, and the institution of caste permits men of different origin and civilization to live side by side without surrendering their treasured racial and cultural identity.

One may question whether a caste or castelike society would accord well with the requirements of modern industry. Industrial societies have hitherto found their principal growth in areas where no differences of race or civilization divided the population into separate compartments. This promoted the circulation of talent from low to high position, and such social mobility undoubtedly made easier and more rapid the progress of industrial development. Yet, in most of the earth, the rise of modern industry has not been associated with racially homogeneous societies. In the non-European countries, wherever Europeans established trading and industrial enterprises on the model of those with which they were familiar at home, it was and remains customary to reserve the managerial and principal technical jobs for fellow-nationals, while using native labor for humbler tasks. A reassertion and extension of this pattern cannot be ruled out of the realm of possibility for the future, though the preserve of a future dominant caste would probably be military duty and public administration, not industrial and commercial enterprise.

Whether a process of blending and assimilation between races and civilizations comes to predominate, or whether the trend may run instead toward the establishment of a new caste system, cannot, I think, be predicted. One pattern might prevail in some parts of the earth, the other in others. Some of the nations and races of mankind might establish an equal partnership while excluding others from the fold. All one can say is that either extreme—complete assimilation among all the racial and cultural varieties of mankind or the conversion of every existing nation into a caste—seems beyond the bounds of probability.

Two things remain to be said. First, one should recognize that either blending or caste segregation constitutes a workable response to the increased mingling of races and civilizations which future political and economic changes seem likely to bring. Nor should one assume that a caste type of society will necessarily repel all but the dominant caste. Men sometimes may prefer to withdraw within a circle of what is familiar and dependable rather than to risk the intense personal difficulties which blending would entail during a long period of transition. And, by providing a sharper focus of loyalty within what might otherwise appear as an almost undifferentiated mass of world society, caste has some positive virtue of its own. Save in the geographical dimension, caste is scarcely different from the nationalism which is so often praised today.

The second point to consider is this. So long as human nature remains more or less unchanged, some lines of social discrimination between alien and fellow seem certain to arise. I suggest that individual men have need of an alien against whom to project their fear and hate, upon whom they may either look down and thus fortify their own self-esteem, or at whom they may look askance, blaming his power or ill-will for whatever hardships or disappointments they may suffer. If, perchance, racial and cultural distinctions should cease to provide such definition between alien and fellow, other lines of social discrimination might have to be invented. Thus I can imagine that a powerful religious movement might arise and preach, as Christianity did under the Roman Empire, the complete insignificance of racial and cultural differences. But the very force of a missionary religion would set up new lines of social demarcation between those who adhered to it and those who did not; and, even should such a religion succeed in converting all mankind, sects and heresies might be expected to arise, reintroducing the distinction between fellow and alien which men seem to find so necessary for their emotional lives.[5]

At any rate, this was the history of Christianity within

5. Even should our imagined dominant power enter the religious arena and use its police power to enforce religious uniformity, some other method of dividing society into in-group and out-group would, I believe, be found. The history of the Byzantine Empire is instructive. When state persecution succeeded in establishing religious and political conformity within the Byzantine heartlands of Asia Minor and the Balkan Peninsula, rival factions arose to distract the life of the capital, this time organized around racing clubs! The "Greens" and the "Blues" not only backed rival horses and rioted in the hippodrome; they also came near to toppling the emperor Justinian from his throne in A.D. 532.

the Roman Empire. By their conversion the first Christians became new men, neither Jew nor Greek nor barbarian. But, as the church grew great, heresies arose to challenge and to break down Christian universality. Moreover, it is worth noting that the principal sects which won enduring success did so within the geographical lines of old racial, national, and cultural units. This suggests that cultural and racial cleavages had not been erased by centuries of Roman rule or truly transcended by religious conversion.

Of all the problems which today confront mankind, the antipathy between races and cultures seems likely to endure the longest and prove the most difficult to handle because it is the most permanently and deeply rooted in human instinct and impulse. Greater mixture between alien peoples seems almost certain to come in the future, but it is far from certain that from such mixing any better understanding or more kindly relationship between the diverse segments of mankind will arise. Rational argument and rational adjustment of laws and relationships between nations and peoples may change the modes of its expression but cannot remove distrust between men of differing appearance and differing customs; and even the far stronger appeal of religion is unlikely to do more than change the symbols by which men distinguish fellow from alien.

7

The Moral Problem.—If events should follow even approximately in the paths suggested above, it is clear that the moral difficulties of mankind will continue to increase in the near future. The brutality of war could be counted upon to blunt human feelings; the uprooting which flight and battle and, perhaps, forced labor might bring to millions upon millions of human beings would weaken habitual moral codes and intensify the confusion between right and wrong, which already exists very widely in the world. Mixture of peoples with varying moral ideas, varying religions, and varying habits and customs would be likely to reach unprecedented levels in the course of a future war; and the sort of postwar settlement I have imagined would not do much to unscramble the resulting social omelet. Rather, increasing political and economic contact across cultural frontiers would result from the institutional changes needful if contemporary military, political, and economic dilemmas are to be effectually overcome. Such contact would, at least initially, forward the process by which established moral standards have already suffered serious erosion.

There is another sense in which any adequate solution of contemporary political problems would increase the moral difficulties men face. This has been mentioned already, but perhaps it deserves fresh emphasis.

On the political level a decay of the national state as a sovereign unit of government would be sure to weaken each individual's self-identification with the particular nation to which he happened to belong. Self-identification with humanity as a whole or with an international organization wielding world power would at best be a pallid substitute for nationalism; and, if service to the nation no longer could command an unambiguous and immediate response as an unquestionably worth-while dedication, then the great problems of the final end of human life and the true values of human existence might assume a more frightening insistency. Few men today feel that the fact that they happen to live in New York, London, Paris, Moscow, or Peking is in itself anything but an accident. That accident certainly does not provide them with a guide to conduct or with a whole, greater than self, which may rightfully demand the service and sacrifice of its separate individual members. Nations now do provide their citizens with an object of devotion, and, in many circumstances, they offer a standard of behavior and a scheme of values—a scheme caricatured, though not past recognition, by the slogan: "My country, right or wrong." It follows that, should nationality become as much a matter of social indifference as residence in a particular city is today, then men would lose an important moral support. They would find themselves forced back more than ever before upon their private personal resources when it came to seeking a moral guide. Conceivably, nations might sink to such unimportance; but, because such disintegration of human groupings is painful, I have already suggested that nations might instead transmute themselves into castelike bodies and still command human loyalty, though not in what we today would easily recognize as a political mold.

The moral effects of an adequate solution of the world's economic problems would be similar. Before the peasant millions of the earth can be persuaded to restrain their procreation within the bounds set by the availability of means of livelihood, radical changes in their ancestral values and customs will be necessary. For instance, it seems certain that a basic alteration of the Chinese family system would be needed. The breeding of sons is traditionally considered a duty by nearly all Chinese in order to assure both that proper reverence be paid to the ancestors and that the parents will have someone to look after them in their old age. Yet it is his identification with his family that serves a Chinese as his main moral guide in life. Any considerable alteration in family tradition would certainly shake Chinese society to its very roots and leave millions upon millions of individuals morally and psychologically adrift. This is but one example of the sort of revolution in social attitudes which might prove necessary before the economic difficulties of our own time and of the future can be met. It follows that, in so far as they are met, one immediate consequence will be to increase moral confusion and uncertainty.

What answers to moral and metaphysical questions may satisfy questing spirits in time to come cannot possibly be forecast. Clearly a world in which local communities had decayed, and in which drastic alteration in age-old family and social traditions had been made, would be ripe for the reception of some religion which would offer men a compelling focus for their loyalty and a clear moral guide for their conduct. But whether such a response to the conditions I have imagined will come at all; whether one or more than one religion may win men's allegiance; whether men may revive one or more than one of the existing religions of the earth or instead adhere to some new religious revelation—these are all questions which can only be asked, not answered.

Without religious revival on a grand scale, I should think it likely that moral lassitude and a spirit of indifference, a sense of futility, and, perhaps, a supine fatalism would increasingly gain hold of men's minds; and, having nothing much worth while to live for or strive for, they might even cease to propagate their kind in sufficient number to prevent a decrease in the population of the earth. Something like this frame of mind did come to possess the Greeks and Romans, and the curious demographic decay of those nations in the days of the Roman Empire may have been connected with the political and religious disintegration of their ancestral way of life.

8

I do not imagine that religion alone would suffice to restore a moral soundness to mankind. If the yeasty fermentation of human society which is in progress today should continue forever, it would be sure to sour any future religious effort at codification of the relations of man to man and of man to the universe. Changes in habits and institutions would continue to outstrip the adjustment of practical moral rules to new conditions, and a widening gap between what men feel ought to prevail and what actually did prevail would continue to confound the best efforts of philosophers and prophets to interpret and evangelize the world.

There is, however, good ground for believing that, should political and economic unification come to the earth, the general pace of social change all round the globe would soon begin to slow down. One consequence of the establishment of an effective international organization would be the growth of a world bureaucracy, and bureaucracies are notoriously conservative. This is what I imagine might happen: During the first fifty to seventy-five years after the establishment of effective international government, there would come a series of radical and rapid changes as local institutions were adjusted to the new shape of world affairs. Pressing economic problems, particularly the population problem, might well require drastic reordering of social habits among vast populations. These things I have already spoken of; and, if the world bureaucrats turned out to be as successful as I think they might be, then, within two or three generations, the various human societies of the earth might begin to arrive at something approaching an even keel. New problems would of course continue to arise, but they might prove manageable within the administrative framework which had been evolved to meet the initial challenges confronting the leaders of the world when they first looked round to survey the ruins left by World War III.

If so, a strong conservatism would almost surely set in among officials and politicians. The more successful the first generations, the more certainly would their successors hallow their example. Every social organization is prone to cling to any particularly successful adjustment it may have achieved and usually does so long after circumstances have changed. Normally, some serious challenge from outside is needful before a successful past can be discredited and at length abandoned or radically modified. But a world-wide international organization would by definition be immune from outside challenge to its power. Hence a mandarin-like immobility might easily overtake the officials who served it, and their grip on economic and political activities would be strong enough to make radical innovation nearly impossible.

On the other hand, it does not seem in the least likely that men will forget the power of deliberate invention which has been so startlingly demonstrated to us in the past one hundred and fifty years. New industrial and agricultural techniques will almost surely continue to be invented as long as scientists and industrial research laboratories remain; and this might be understood to assure an indefinite continuance of technical—and through technical of social—change. Perhaps so; but there is a difference between laboratory invention and practical application which might well prove far harder to surmount under future conditions than it is today. Good reasons can almost always be found for not trying something new on an industrial scale. Corporations today repress patents in order to protect their interest in some older, less efficient process; in the future, nations might do the same. Labor unions today resist the introduction of labor-saving devices and methods in order to protect the skills and employment of their members; in the future, whole peoples might behave analogously.

More than this, it is often possible to argue that the introduction of some new technique will cost more in terms of social disruption and human displacement than it is really worth. This argument was used against the introduction of the mechanical cotton-picker in the southern United States during the 1930's; and, even without the unemployment which then prevailed, one can imagine some judicious social engineer of the future shaking his head sagely when he seeks to balance the human costs of depriving some millions of men of their accustomed work against the saving in cost which some new machine or method might bring—and coming to the conclusion that, while a cautious and gradual shift extending over long years might be advisable, further studies should be made before any action is taken. Such bureaucratic wisdom, combined with the resistance to radical innovation which both industrial managers and workmen may be counted upon to exhibit, might drastically reduce the impact of inventions upon society and, in doing so, would slow down the action of one of the principal contemporary springs of social change.

Finally, the abolition of international war would remove what is today perhaps the most potent single factor in promoting and accelerating social change—one which, I argued in chapter ii, has played a distinguished role in human history since at least 2000 B.C.

These considerations lead me to suppose that the world of the future will probably not indefinitely maintain the dizzying pace of social change which we now experience. Change would presumably still come, partly from the interaction of varying civilizations, partly from industrial invention, partly from artistic and religious invention. It might well happen that the most active and significant sector of social change would come to reside in these latter fields of human activity; for art and religion are, by their very nature, less subject to the paralyzing hand of a conservative bureaucracy. On the other hand, without the stimulus of constant political and economic upheaval, it might happen that men would eventually settle down to almost fixed art forms and almost fixed beliefs and that further artistic and intellectual history would be limited to ringing the changes on certain established themes.

Speculation of this sort verges on the ridiculous. Only time will tell whether human society is destined to settle down to what might be called a "culture civilization" girdling the globe, with its political, economic, and cul-

tural forms even more fixed and stable than were the forms
of the Roman Empire or the Chinese Empire; or whether
some new upheaval of the human spirit may cause men to
press forward in directions yet unimagined and un-
imaginable.

Historical analogies for the sort of world society I have
described leap at once to mind. As Toynbee has pointed
out, many civilizations in the past have, after a period of
fratricidal strife, seen the establishment of a single governmental unit embracing the whole area of the civilization.
There was Rome; and, before Rome, Persia; before Persia,
Assyria; before Assyria, Babylonia and the New Empire of
Egypt. Each in its time conquered the civilized world and
established what Toynbee has called a "universal state."
Other civilizations, genetically unrelated to our own, have
experienced what appear to be analogous developments.
These facts make it seem the more probable that a Western
universal state is now on the way; and since, as no earlier
civilization has, the West has been able to extend its
tentacles over the whole terrestrial globe, any conceivable
universal state for Western civilization will be truly and
in the full geographical sense a world state.

Resort to historical analogy suggests the ultimate possibility of decline and disruption. Each of the universal states
of the past waxed mighy for a day and then decayed. May
we anticipate a similar fate for a universal state that would
embrace the whole globe?

I do not think such a question can be answered. Obviously, the further one seeks to project one's imagination into
the future, the greater the uncertainty and the larger the

margin of probable error. Yet this much does seem clear: the pattern of decline and fall could never be the same. Rome and the other universal states of the past were overthrown partly by internal decay, partly by attack from outside. But in a world state there would be no outside, unless the fishes of the sea or the insects of the earth should attack. It is quite inconceivable that any barabarous people lurking in some odd corner of the world could overthrow a society possessed of the power which modern industrial technology gives.

Against internal decay there can be no guaranty. Rome's internal breakup was a complicated transformation; but the decisive political change lay in the fact that after the time of Diocletian the Roman government could no longer command the tax moneys necessary to pay the bureaucracy and so had to resort to payment in kind, and particularly to payment by grant of usufruct of land. The great officials of the Roman Empire thus found themselves no longer dependent on the central authority for their income, drawing it directly from estates which they were able to treat as private property. As a consequence obedience to the central authority ceased to be necessary, and the path was cleared for a devolution of political power which in western Europe resulted at last in the fragmentation of feudalism. In an industrial society such a development seems inconceivable. As long as the techniques of industrial production are not forgotten, the wealth of the world will be sufficient to support, and tax income will be sufficient to pay, officials and soldiers essential to an international government.

Stretching the imagination through long vistas of time,

one can conceive that geological or geographical changes might upset the equipoise of the world. Exhaustion of mineral resources, for example, or the cooling of the earth, might create a crisis of the first magnitude. Biological changes resulting in a steady diminution of population or in a decline in human intelligence might undermine world society and in due course bring it crumbling to the ground. But, short of such changes, it is hard to see what necessity would bring about a decline and fall.

Of these, the population factor seems the only candidate likely to operate in what we are accustomed to think of as historical time. Decline of population was an important influence in weakening the power of Rome, and it is a disturbing fact that the most highly industrialized modern societies have shown a tendency for population growth to slack off. If nothing should interrupt the trend, an eventual decline might someday set in. Conceivably, population decline might spread to all the societies of the earth if the entire world were to become industrialized or adjusted to a standard of living based upon an industrial economy. But it seems equally possible that a biological balance might re-establish itself as habits and customs became better adjusted to industrial living, so that decline would automatically be averted. Indeed, if population shrinkage should seem a serious problem, our future world authority might as a matter of policy institute rewards for parenthood which would be great enough to counteract any incipient decline. Thus it does not seem that this threat to the indefinite continuance of a world order would be great.

Much more probable would be a slow undulation of economic and cultural leadership from one area of the world to another. The nation which emerged victor from a third world war might very well go the way of Rome in the sense that the economic and perhaps also the biological basis of its power might gradually wane. The citizens of such a nation would probably at first predominate in the military forces of the international organization and might spend long years stationed in far corners of the earth. They might also at first predominate in the civil administration of international government and would be tempted to take unto themselves the perquisites and pleasures of a ruling caste. Under such conditions lavish expenditure and conspicuous consumption might become the way of life of a majority of the citizens of the dominant power. The temptation to abandon the hard and dirty work of farm and factory would certainly be great; yet never in history, I believe, has a ruling class which took up a plunderer's way of life maintained itself biologically. It follows that, in proportion as manpower was drained from productive work into military and administrative occupations, the industrial strength and pre-eminence of our hypothetical dominant power would be likely to shrink. Such was in fact very much the fate of Italy, whose inhabitants conquered the Mediterranean world in the first century B.C. and then left the fields and the workshops to foreign slaves.

Such a dissipation and decay on the part of a victor nation would not be inevitable. Much would depend on the wisdom and restraint with which power was exercised; on the restraints that might be imposed on the representatives of the dominant power in dealings with the other peoples of the world; on the degree to which co-operation and not compulsion were used to secure international stability—

in other words, on the degree to which the wishes of the less powerful nations and peoples were taken into consideration. Much, too, would depend on the proportion of a dominant power's total manpower drawn into military and administrative careers, and this in turn would depend in part on the state of the world and on the amount of compulsion and supervision judged necessary.

In general, the greater the measure of conquest, the more a dominant power would suffer from the privileges which it arrogated to its citizens; and the greater the measure of voluntary co-operation and of consideration for the rights and wishes of other peoples, the less the dominant power would in the end suffer from the corruption of its own citizens.

An ideal future world state, it seems to me, would be a genuinely democratic one, in which all the inhabitants of the earth were able and willing to take an equal part in determining the policies of governmental authorities. But I believe that such an ideal can never be realized. Before a democratic international government could function, the pitfalls of racial and cultural antagonism and the confusion and divergence of contemporary moral systems would first have somehow to be overcome. I have already suggested some of the obstacles. Moreover, the technicality of government business is great enough already and is likely to become greater in future as the sphere of governmental activity expands over larger geographic areas and cuts a wider swath through economic and social affairs. Few ordinary men are capable and have the chance of educating themselves to the point of understanding such technicalities; and, without a reasonably well-informed and judicious electorate, democratic control of the machine of government must become part farce, part fraud. This trend is already apparent in the democratic parliamentary nation-states of western Europe and America; it would be far more pronounced in any system of administration that took the whole world for its province.

It seems clear that any future world administration would have to start, like the League of Nations and the United Nations, as a government of experts, responsible in theory to a council of official representatives of the nation-states of the world, and responsible in fact largely to the national authorities of a dominant power. Democratic control over such a body would be remote indeed, and, while further evolution in a democratic direction might prove possible, I have little faith that it would in fact occur.

Unless a wide consensus among all the peoples of the earth could somehow establish itself, truly democratic control of world administration would simply break down from lack of a united, supreme will. But it seems unlikely that men will ever so bury their differences as to arrive at such a universal consensus. A government of officials, tolerating, always willing to consult, and sometimes ready to defer to national representative bodies seems the best that can be expected of a future world administration. A dictatorship whose officials received orders only from above would be the worst. An actual world administration, if it should come to pass, would no doubt fall somewhere between the best and the worst.

No one will feel that this description of a future world makes what may lie before us seem altogether inviting or much of an improvement on the past. Gains would be matched by losses, peace dulled by conformity, security spoiled by ennui. Yet we cannot stand still; even less can we return to some period of the world's past. The question of what to do about the state of human affairs—if they were, are, and will be anything like what has here been written down—is peculiarly pressing for Americans and is less so for other peoples only because their present and future responsibilities are likely to be less than those falling and about to fall on American shoulders. What Americans in this generation ought to do will be considered in the next chapter.

CHAPTER FIVE

WHAT IS TO BE DONE?

1

Men of good will can find little to encourage them in the present state of international relations, and the future promises to become worse before it can become better. The United States will inevitably have a tremendous role to play in what is to come; and, as long as democratic institutions exist in this country, the policies of the government will bear a fairly direct relation to the attitudes, opinions, and votes of the American people. Thus tremendous responsibility and tremendous opportunity lie upon us all. What are we to do? What *should* we do?

Three general attitudes toward the future seem possible. One may look out upon the world and conclude that all possible alternatives are evil; that the world is stupidly and cruelly managed today and promises to be worse run in time to come. Perhaps, then, the best possible course is to attend to the intimate relations of private life, trying within that limited sphere to foster harmony and human kindness and in general to lead as good and satisfying a life as may be possible amid the storms of civil and international society. To some, such a withdrawal from public affairs may seem defeatism; but it can be defended, as religious movements have always been defended, by arguing that, if everyone in the world went and did likewise, most or all of the social and political problems which distract mankind would either fade away or be raised to the level of peaceable compromise and adjustment.

It is also possible to refuse to believe that conditions of the past will never come again. Men who remember their youth and feel that things as they were then were normal and right are greatly tempted to consider all the threats and portents of our time as an inconvenient interruption in the normal state of human affairs. They trust that, by making a few concessions in diplomatic negotiations and a few reforms at home, present conflicts will gradually subside and a gradual stabilization within each nation-state and between them will come to pass. It is easy to ridicule such ideas as ostrich-like, Blimpish, or what have you; yet the policy of muddling through, hoping for the best, and clinging to established loyalties and institutions is not always unwise. Many storms blow over, and many dire predictions go unfulfilled. To see future dangers too clearly is sometimes a great handicap, paralyzing resolution and weakening action. Against such possibility, the stubbornly conservative mind may serve as a valuable counterweight.

A third possible reaction to the present state of the world is to try to change and reform it. All too often reformers fail to pay due attention to the limits of practical possibility and are unjustifiably confident of the accuracy of their foresight. When that is the case, they win the disregard of practical men and perhaps deserve it. On the other hand, in time of severe crisis practical men may easily find themselves at a loss to know what to do next. Reformers and visionaries then have their chance, and the public welfare will depend upon how sound and wise their visions prove to be. A healthy society needs both wings: the conservative and the radical, the practical man and the visionary; and, if each can appreciate the social value of the other, so much the better.

Obviously this book is not addressed to persons who wish to retreat into private life, nor can it seem anything but nonsense to those who feel that existing institutions are generally adequate to the world's needs. Reformers and visionaries, however, ought to respond to the picture of a future world from which war and economic distress have both been removed. Certainly the abolition of war is not an unworthy ideal, and to strive for an organization of the world capable of bringing peace, plenty, and security is not ignoble. The difficulty is that such a happy outcome seems only to emerge dimly from seas of blood and tears yet to be shed; and many will ask themselves whether the end can possibly justify the means, whether the hope of a better society would not in reality be snuffed out by the bloody hands of tyrants, whose power, even if world wide, would serve none but selfish and evil purposes.

Such an outcome of fresh wars is certainly a danger; and if (though I think it improbable), not one, but a long series of further international wars should lie ahead of humanity, then I believe that a world tyrant, like Caesar, might finally arise to end both international warfare and individual liberty. Decisions made from day to day will have much to do with whether such an outcome blasts the more happy future which I think possible, and in particular the acts and attitudes of the American people and government will have much to do with deciding the question.

The position in which the American people find themselves in 1953 is peculiarly difficult. For eight years or more both people and government in the United States have been inspired by a fundamentally conservative spirit. The desire to return to normal, to get Europe back on its feet, to check world revolution, to establish a world balance which will allow Americans to look after their own affairs in peace while the other nations of the earth do the same—these have been the aims of American foreign policy. Yet the result has been the establishment of new and ever more entangling alliances; and, ironically, the pursuit of peace and quiet led the United States to the forefront of a difficult diplomatic struggle and persuaded the government not only to undertake an expensive armaments race with the Soviet Union but also to engage in a trying war in Korea. This was not what Americans expected. With hopes betrayed, it is hard to avoid anger and bewilderment.

A truer intellectual vision of what has happened and is happening and will likely happen in time to come may help to remove some of this anger and bewilderment. If the leaders of American opinion can be brought to recognize that transnational organization on the model of NATO and SHAPE has come into the world not simply because of the wickedness of the men in the Kremlin (or in the White House) but because separate nations can no longer protect themselves, then petulence with allies and unreasoned anger against the Russians would diminish, and the free world would gain in stability and strength. Similarly, if Americans could raise their minds above the limits set by established national frontiers and admit that the economic welfare of all the nations of the free world is of high concern to each—and of concern especially to the hub and

center of it all, the United States—then more equable transnational economic policies could be introduced and old
ones followed with a stronger assurance of continued support from Congress and the American public.

Finally, if Americans could come to believe that the only
satisfactory long-term solution of the world's political and
economic problems would be the establishment of a world-
wide international organization, sufficiently powerful to
keep the peace and sufficiently energetic to undertake economic readjustment on a global basis—if Americans could
hold steadily before themselves such a vision of a possible
future, they would have a goal worthy to be striven for
with high heart. Such a goal, I believe, would be more nearly attainable and more truly in accord with the current of
contemporary history than is our present effort to return to
a "normal" which in part never existed and in part has
vanished irreparably in the smoke of two world wars.

Two objections to such a program immediately arise.
On the one hand, it can truly be said and should frankly be
admitted that any advance toward a greater unification of
the world will involve real losses and damages to the human
spirit. I have already touched upon the moral problems
which would be enhanced by a diminution of national political ties and by a mixing of peoples. The likelihood of a
dead level of uniformity all round the world may, I think, be
discounted; but the danger that ill-will among races and
civilizations might continue and that in the long run a
bureaucratic rigidity might damp human progress does
seem real. If, then, world peace and prosperity are likely to
bring these failures in their train, why pursue a future in
which good and bad are so irretrievably mixed?

In reply, one may say simply that human affairs always exhibit such an alloy of gain and loss, good and evil, advance and retrogression. To him who insists upon perfection, all action becomes repellant. The only thing for such a man to do is to retreat from the world of men—in itself, surely, a mixed blessing.

Perhaps crusading faith can flourish only on a doctrine of perfectability. If so, it must be a deception and will sooner or later mislead and disappoint its devotees. A wide-eyed appreciation of likely dangers and probable evils should prepare men to avoid at least the worst of the pitfalls ahead and might even give our descendants a fighting chance to escape unscathed by finding humane and liberal solutions to the moral and cultural conflicts which beset, and will continue to beset, human society throughout the foreseeable future.

At any rate, it seems quite obvious to me that the problems of peace and plenty are the first and most urgent tasks confronting the present generation of mankind. The sooner they can be solved reasonably well, the sooner men will be free to turn attention to more difficult and perhaps more important problems. But until a world-wide authority can be established, and until such an authority can prevent war and relieve the most critical economic disbalances of the world, the moral conflicts of our time and the clash of civilizations and races will simply fester and grow worse. Whether men of some future generation will be able to solve such problems—and other problems we do not yet even imagine—can surely remain for us an academic exercise of the imagination. Not to be mindful of the reality of the more ultimate problems which confront mankind would certainly be folly; to allow doubts and hesitations about their future solution to prevent our own grappling with the world's current political and economic problems would also be folly. If we and our children can manfully do our part, perhaps it can safely be left to our remoter descendants to equal, or fail to equal, our achievement on the quite different planes of human action which will remain to challenge their wisdom and kindliness, even should men of the twentieth century achieve all I have argued may be possible for them.

A second objection to the ideal goal of American international policy suggested above takes the form of a *reductio ad absurdam*. If World War III is on the way, why not get it over with now or, at any rate, as soon as possible? If an international organization dominated by a single great power is historically predestined, why not start at once to turn the United States into that power, since it is so much more pleasant to rule than to be ruled? Why not, in short, embark immediately upon an all-out mobilization and, when our preparation is complete, then deliberately provoke a war with Russia, thus putting an end to the uncertainty and half-measures of cold war?

Such a course can recommend itself to no one who is not blind with rage or so greedy for power as to be unworthy of it. Hitler's example is not acceptable to anyone who cherishes the ideals of Western civilization and who takes the American national tradition seriously.

Nor would such an aggressive and imperialistic policy be very likely to succeed, even in the narrow military sense. Allies would scarcely be available, a bad consience at home would surely weaken America's own war effort, and one might expect the Russians and their allies to fight as heroically as they in fact fought against Hitler. Even should such an America conquer, it would fit itself only for a tyrant's role over the rest of mankind. Such a role would be repellant to all Americans. Such conquest and tyranny would certainly involve the destruction of our own domestic institutions and most cherished traditions, for a foreign tyrant would also have to become a tyrant at home. Finally, I have already argued that it is only reasonable to expect the penalties of tyranny to undermine and sooner or later to overthrow the power of such a conqueror of the earth.

As things stand today, I believe that there are good and persuasive reasons for believing that the United States would make a better dominant power than would Soviet Russia. To be sure, the question as to whether our success is to be preferred to that of the Russians is really prejudged for an American, and doubtless I am profoundly biased. But for the world at large the question is real and urgent, and upon the choice of other peoples may well depend the eventual outcome of the contest.

If we try to put away nationalistic feeling for a moment and look upon ourselves as others see us, how does the image we present compare with that of the Soviet Union? For all our differences, we share with the Russians at least a verbal adherence to very similar ideals. Liberty and democracy, peace and abundance, the fullest possible development of the individual person, all these are as much a part of the official Communist program as they are of the American liberal dream. We differ from the Russians theoretically concerning the means by which it is hoped that these ideals can be realized; we differ from them practically in the manner and degree with which we and they fail to realize ideals in daily life.

These differences are of the highest importance. Communists profess that the end justifies any means. Chicanery, deceit, violence, and bloodshed are all acceptable so long as they are designed to forward the advance of communism and—in the short run—to increase the power and security of the Soviet state. But if there is any truth about human life which is incontrovertable it is this: daily actions, habits, and attitudes control and guide future development. It is from today's actual practice that future evolution inevitably begins; and the defects of human wisdom are such that ideals and ultimate goals have an uncomfortable way of receding forever and forever exactly in proportion as daily actions fall short of the ideal. The reality of the future is therefore certain to take a strong color from the practices and shortcomings of the ages preceding.

No more striking example of this historical continuity could be found than that offered by the likenesses and continuities between czarist and Stalinist Russia. The ideals of communism are certainly different from those of czarist Russia, and it would be wrong to say that those ideals have had no influence on practice. But there has been a process of selection: only the aspects of Communist principles that could easily be made to accord with czarist practice have been acted upon, and the rest of the ideal has been postponed to an indefinite future when all things will, according to official doctrine, somehow be made new. In fact, though, national character, customs, and institutions have a tremendous toughness and resilience. Even the fires of revolution and temporary social disintegration are not enough to destroy them, or even perhaps to alter them greatly.

One may therefore expect some survival of the differences in practice and institutions which now distinguish the Soviet Union from the United States, no matter what radical changes the future may bring to one or both. And if one asks which of the two societies now comes the nearer to living up in practice to the ideals both profess in theory, there can, I think, be only one answer. The United States is freer, less brutal, more civilized than the Soviet Union. America is richer and can afford to be more generous in material things. American society is more stable and can afford to be more tolerant of diversity in opinion and behavior. And, perhaps not least in the eyes of other peoples, we Americans are less eager for world power than the masters of the Kremlin appear to be. Americans are less willing to use violence than Bolshevik leaders have been, and they are far less certain that they know the whole Truth for all Mankind—a truth which the rulers of Russia profess to find embalmed in sacred texts from the pens of Marx, Lenin, and (at least until recently) Stalin.

Despite the brutalizing effect which a third world war would undoubtedly have upon American life, despite impoverishment, internal strains, and limitation of individual liberty which a long and difficult war would certainly entail, one may confidently expect a survival of at least a part of the margin which now exists between the Russians and ourselves. War would have the effect of implanting all the deeper the dark and abominable traits of the present Russian government and would make them all the more difficult to slough off afterward. War would certainly damage American society, but it could not eradicate all traces of liberal practice and might even leave our institutions essentially undamaged as was the case with the first two World Wars. Predictions were freely made in the late 1930's that American participation in a great war would lead to dictatorship and revolution, but it did not turn out so. Similar predictions made with respect to a future war must therefore be discounted. Dictatorship might come, but it might not; and, if the American people remain steadfast, it will not.

Against the massive force of use and wont, the warm ideals of Communist or of liberal theory can have only a limited effect. Actual practice counts for more; and, inasmuch as the United States comes closer to liberal ideals than the Soviet Union does to Communist ones, it seems legitimate to conclude that American world leadership would be better, more liberating, more tolerable for the world than would Russian Communist victory.

On the other hand, should the United States so betray itself as deliberately to provoke a war with the aim of winning hegemony over the entire globe, a heavy and irreparable blow would be dealt to our claim to rank morally above the Russian state. Such a path would, indeed, be an imitation of Communist practice in the sense that it would seek to justify proximate evil by ultimate good; and, should the United States act on such principles, the betrayal of any hoped-for good could certainly be expected from our hands, as Marxian ideals are today betrayed by the Russian Communists.

There is a final reason for refusing to consider launching a preventive war at our earliest convenience. Although a third world war seems likely, and although preparation to withstand a war is a vital necessity, yet no one can say with complete and final certainty that war will actually come. There is a chance that things will turn out differently, and, as long as the chance remains, it should most emphatically be cherished. One can imagine, for example, that some future Russian government might decide to come to terms without war. One can hope that international control of atomic weapons might be established under the United Nations after all; one can detect the faint possibility of the creation of international armed force through the "negotiation from strength" of which American official spokesmen have sometimes hopefully talked.

Before such a change could come about, the nations of the free world would have to win such indefeasible military strength, such unity among themselves, such patent economic stability and prosperity, such self-assurance and inner harmony as to make their collapse or military defeat clearly impossible. Probably, too, a series of troubles within the Communist world would be necessary. If the Russians and their satellites should experience persistent failures to meet military and economic goals; if friction between nations and between classes within the Communist fold became acute; if uncertainties about the adequacy and accuracy of Stalinist dogma gained ground; if Communist officials began to feel scruples about the ruthless means they habitually employ against the common people under them; and if the oppressed classes began to show serious discontent with their lot—if such signs and portents of Communist weakness and failure should multiply, then perhaps a negotiated settlement could really be achieved, and men might even rise to the point of achieving a pacification of the world through agreement rather than through force. Who can say that these things are altogether impossible? Who can say that Communist tyranny and deceit will endure all the strains arising from within over a period of decades or even generations? While so happy an outcome of the present condition of the world does not seem likely, if it is possible at all, it would surely be worth waiting for. Worth waiting a long time for.

2

No matter what may lie ahead, the American people and government should seek to strengthen and broaden the transnational association which is the free world. In the short run this would bolster our national security and prosperity; in the long run, such a policy, if successfully pursued, would, I believe, convert the free world into the kernel of a future world-wide international government.

In such a process there are bound to be ups and downs. Many ambitious and forward-looking plans are sure to fail or fall short, as the hope for a European army seems to be falling short in the summer of 1953. It may even happen that the bonds which today unite the members of the North Atlantic Treaty Organization and the ties that hold Russian satellites to Moscow may weaken, or, in some cases, dissolve entirely. National feuds and jealousies on both sides of the iron curtain are very deep and cannot be overcome all at once; and it is not difficult to imagine circumstances in which Communist maneuvers and atavistic appeals to nationalism might succeed in disrupting much that seemed to have been accomplished among the nations of the free world toward building a firm transnational structure of military and economic administration.

There is, indeed, a tragic irony in the fact that, the more peaceably we and the Russians behave toward one another, the more stubborn will the obstacles to any reshaping of the world's institutions that could really and permanently end international war become. Yet I am convinced of this: even should peace temporarily break out between the Communist and the free worlds and permit a return to plural national sovereignties in Europe and elsewhere, such a reversion to familiar political forms would turn out to be no more than an interlude. Sooner or later independent sovereign states have always gone to war in the past; if they do so in the future, all the forces encouraging transnational administration would once more be unleashed, presumably with strength increased as much over what prevailed during World War II as the transnational administration of World War II itself represented an advance over the practices of World War I.

It is always sobering to remember that what may happen to the United States in the next two or three decades depends only in part upon our own action and attitudes. Yet, in international affairs, it is our own national behavior which we most nearly control, and the direction and emphasis of American foreign policy will certainly count for much. If we can avoid a return to irritable isolationism and at the same time refrain from violent coercion of our allies, and if we can work steadily at the task of transforming the free world from a slogan into a fact, then, I think, the American share in fixing the course of future history will be great indeed.

In Europe a judicious mixture of forbearance with diplomatic firmness in support of NATO and its associated transnational organizations may yet win through. Up to 1953, progress has been heartening in spite of all difficulties. What has already been done would have seemed beyond the bounds of reasonable possibility only six years ago. If such growth can be maintained, after twenty or thirty years the United States will find itself the leader of a firm and coherent military and economic community, spanning the North Atlantic and uniting the heartland of North America with the historic center of Western civilization. Such a community would be powerful indeed, and war, far from disrupting it, would most likely unite the community still more closely. This must surely be the primary goal for which the American people ought to strive in foreign affairs. Hope and faith in ourselves and in our allies may do much; vigorous effort can do more. Obstacles can be overcome if the will and the necessary understanding to grapple with them can be found.

The situation in Asia and the Middle East is much more precarious. The free world's organization in those parts, where it exists at all, is tenuous in the extreme. Obstacles to the co-operative creation of military and economic bulwarks against further Communist advance are much greater than those which confront us in Europe. But to take the attitude that nothing can be done is rank defeatism. It would be a refusal of the vocation to world leadership; and such a refusal might well turn out to be an abdication in favor of the Soviet Union, whose appetite for world power can scarcely be doubted, and whose effort has so far been unsparing.

If a peaceable, harmonious, and effective transnational co-operation within the free world can arise to unite western Europe with the United States, and the rest of the non-Communist world with the Atlantic community, then the possibility of peaceable negotiation and eventual settlement with Russia would be vastly increased. At the least, the position of the free world in the cold war would be unassailable, and, if a third world war should come, victory would assuredly rest in our camp. Hence, whatever view one takes of future probability and possibility, a serious and prolonged and massive effort to knit the raveled fringes of the free world into an effective whole is eminently worth while.

At the same time, to assume that American good will and generous intentions will by themselves assure success would be foolish. Our hopes may well be thwarted and our efforts may fail. Indeed, when one remembers the distrust and ill will which now divide Asian and Moslem nations from the West, when one reflects upon the gulfs which exist between our own civilization and that of the non-Western portions of the earth, and when one considers the acute internal problems which distract the peoples of the Far and Middle East, it must be confessed that any solid success for an American-inspired effort to establish military and economic co-operation with Moslem and Asian peoples seems out of the question. But there are halfway houses between complete success and complete failure; Asian neutrality would be better than Asian hostility; and even a halting and halfhearted Asian co-operation would be better than strict neutrality. It is a question of doing what we can to beat down suspicion, while extending aid in a fashion which will help to meet the military and economic difficulties of Asia without arousing the nationalistic hostility of the Asian peoples.

In spite of all Americans and Europeans can do, it must be recognized that communism may yet win fresh victories in Asia and the Middle East. A third world war might take the form of a battle between the Atlantic community, assisted by countries like Australia and Japan, and a Communist-dominated Eurasia. Yet, even should such a disastrous event come to pass, the fact that the United States had made a serious effort to bring the various peoples and nations of the whole non-Communist world into a working partnership might not be totally in vain. Memories of American efforts might persist in Asian nations and encourage defection to our camp. Even more important, the American people would have shown themselves qualified to lead the world to a better, more peaceable, and more prosperous condition; and, should victory be ours, we might then be able to take up where we had been interrupted. An America which had schooled itself in the responsibilities of international leadership during a long cold war would stand a good chance of avoiding the excesses of violence and tyranny which a mere military conqueror would find tempting. Such an America might be able to establish a liberal, co-operative, civilized world order in which all mankind could find a spiritual as well as a physical home.

Thus it appears that the test of American fitness to survive in a cold war and the test of American fitness to lead the world after victory in a third world war are one and the same. The broader and more generous our view, the less we fall back upon an irritable Americanism; the more we strive to make the free world into a single, interdependent whole, the less we hope or imagine that return to the comfortable isolation of the nineteenth century is possible—in short, the more we can look forward and the less we look back, the better our chances to forestall the Russians and, even more important, the better our chances to establish a post–World War III world that a civilized man might care to live in.

American domestic policy should also be a matter of concern. It is imperative that a new depression, comparable to that of the 1930's, be avoided. Any such disaster would surely open wide the gates to communism and would vindicate, or seem to vindicate, Marxian economic prophecy. The experience of the second World War showed what American production can accomplish when all financial and other traditional restraints are removed. Perhaps a long-continued effort at such a pitch would be impossible; but there seems no reason why the rate of expansion and stability of employment and production which has prevailed since 1945 could not be maintained indefinitely. Governmental fiscal manipulation, perhaps additional devices for assuring a continuance of employment and production, may prove needful to assure such a result. Not to find them and use them would be colossal folly; and, indeed, as long as armaments production continues at a rapid rate, and as long as financial assistance to other nations continues to be the highest wisdom, it seems unlikely that any effort to return American economic policy to the laissez faire of earlier generations will be made. As long as the cold war lasts, an American depression does not therefore seem a serious danger.

The question of civil rights for individual citizens is another important and difficult matter. Traditionally, Americans have tolerated the right of individuals to differ from their fellows within relatively wide limits. Communist methods of infiltration and espionage may sometimes take advantage of such tolerance; yet the damage that may so be done is easy to exaggerate. The most important military data about the free world are regularly published in newspapers and government documents. Any other policy would require secrecy not only against the Russians but against ourselves, and no American would wish to hand over the direction of our affairs to an officialdom of secrets.

The best protection from Communist infiltration and espionage is surely to present a strong and vigorous society to Russian inspection. The appeal of Communist doctrine would then be limited to a tiny body of malcontents whose practical power to infiltrate government, labor unions, or other power-wielding bodies would be very small. The best of all possible ways to discredit Communist propaganda is to prove it false by our acts; the best of all possible ways to counter Communist threats is to develop a national and transnational strength that no threat can destroy.

Yet we are not perfect and are never likely to be so. The question of whether Communists should be free to play upon our weaknesses, doing their best to inflame domestic social conflicts and to worsen frictions between the nations of the free world, is not easy to answer. Legal penalties against Communist organizations can assuredly reduce the scope of Communist propaganda by making its dissemination more difficult. On the other hand, there is a standing temptation to use such legal repression to suppress honest criticism of social conditions which, if unremedied, might become sources of weakness. It is easy to dub anyone with whom you disagree a "Communist"; and, in an atmosphere of fear and hate, politicians and juries may apply legal penalties against such dissenters, regardless of whether they are in fact associated with Russian-dominated Communist organizations.

Personally, it does not seem to me that the free world is sufficiently stable, powerful, and prosperous to be able to allow Communists free rein in every part and under every condition. To suppose that a British standard of civil liberty can exist in every part of the free world would be to suppose that every nation has attained the social cohesion and moderation which distinguishes the British from nearly all other peoples. Varying legal measures against Communist organizations will be needed in different countries; and the only guide that can be followed is always to err slightly on the liberal side and to resort to repression only when Communist obstruction is clearly effective. Repression as a substitute for reform is almost sure to be fatal; repression as a prelude and accompaniment to reform may sometimes be necessary, as, for instance, when Communist-led guerrilla war attacks the whole life of a nation.

One of the greatest weaknesses of the United States as potential leader of the peoples of the earth is our domestic attitude toward Negroes and other colored peoples. The greater part of the inhabitants of the earth, after all, do not have white skins; and for them American professions of liberal principles cannot but seem a hollow sham. Race feeling is, unfortunately, not easily overcome, but it does lie within the power of the American people to reduce the harsher and more obviously unjust expressions of race feeling which now disfigure our society. Legal changes can accomplish something; governmental policies can also help. But the fundamental change must occur in the conduct of private persons in their daily lives, a realm where government and laws are nearly powerless, but where each individual American can play a part.

In proportion as Americans and other citizens of the free world prove themselves able to act along the lines here sketched out, the free world will become a better place to live in than it now is. That by itself would go far toward assuring success against communism. The contest for the leadership of the world will be decided only in part by weight of metal and size of armies. The contentment and resolution of the American people and of our allies, the moral conviction with which we act, the clarity of the contrast between Russian Communist conduct and our own way of life, the superior flexibility and democracy of our form of government, and the success with which the United States may prove able to make allies into willing partners sharing in a common enterprise—these factors will have a great deal to do with the outcome of the struggle, whatever form it may take in years to come. Only by maintaining the central values of the liberal tradition, and by improving steadily upon our practice at home and abroad, can the American people make the most of our opportunities and assure our success, sooner or later, in the difficult and trying contest upon which we have entered.

In matters of internal and national policy it is always worth reminding ourselves that, unlike the situation in some other nations, in the United States it is the people at large who have the final say. Political leaders and governmental organizations can take a limited initiative and may sometimes crystallize public opinion by their words or deeds, but they are nonetheless held in check or goaded on by the currents which sweep the public. This means that each individual among us plays his own tiny part in determining what shall and shall not be done, and the success of American policy and its wisdom can be little if at all greater than the wisdom and understanding of the people at large.

Blank defeatism is therefore an unpardonable lack of self-confidence and a confession of ignorance and stupidity. Marxists and the Russians do everything they can to foster the idea that there is an inevitable drift of history in their favor. They preach a revolution written in the stars and in the material relations of production and proclaim that the growing strength of the Soviet state will in time become irresistible while the rotten social fabric of other nations crumbles into the dust. Yet it is the people of the United States who alone can determine whether the social fabric we have inherited will decay and dissolve into hostile fragments. Undue individual selfishness, stubborn class or group loyalties, unbending national pride, or complacent satisfaction with things as they have been in the past might result in destroying the vigor of the United States; but it lies within our power of thought and feeling to prevent such things from occurring. Historical materialism and dialectical necessity are gross oversimplifications of history and of the human spirit. Ideas and ideals play a great part in human events; and, if Americans shape their minds and hearts wisely and well, our chance of success against the Communists seems good. Only a failure of will and intelligence on the part of the American people will make Soviet victory inevitable.

One may nonetheless wonder whether we are equal to the tasks before us. Nations and peoples in the past have sometimes failed to meet the challenges which changing historical conditions thrust upon them and paid the price in defeat or eclipse or slow decay. Penetrating vision and the faith and energy required to act upon such vision are and will be required if the United States is to avoid such a downward path. Much has been accomplished in the last ten years, but all too often it has been accomplished in an irritable, piecemeal, half-blind spirit. Clearer thought and a more definitely sustained will must be brought to bear if the United States is to win through to the world leadership which seems, at least to me, to beckon us onward.

A hundred years ago Karl Marx looked at the rough beginnings of modern industrialism in western Europe and concluded that peaceable adjustment of the conflicts of interest he saw around him would be impossible; and on this basis he elaborated his theory of class struggle and the inevitable victory of the proletariat. But the course of events in the leading industrial nations has not borne out his prophecy very well. There have been class conflicts, and they continue to exist; but a process of compromise and adjustment has taken place in all the Western nations whereby a relatively harmonious industrial society has emerged.

The great problem before civilized societies today is not class but international war. For this Marxist theory offers the dreamed-of brotherhood of the workers of the world. That the theory is not easy to apply has been demonstrated by the quarrels between the Cominform and Yugoslavia. Spontaneous brotherhood cannot be expected to spring even from common theoretical principles; there must also be an organization with supreme power to enforce decisions on disputed points.

Thus the question is: Whose power and what organization will be able to achieve effective supremacy in the earth? The apocalyptic certainty of their eventual success which Communists like to fall back on is a myth. It is a powerful myth which lends the adherents of international communism much needed psychological support when they measure themselves against the obstacles in their path. But there is no need for others who do not accept the theories of Marx or the doctrines and practices of the Russian Communist state to take such a myth very seriously. It lies within our power to disprove Communist claims by continuing to make prudent, wise reforms and by taking vigilant, effective precautions against sudden attack.

If we too can school ourselves to think in long terms and to imagine a world from which the possibility of war has vanished and, with an awareness of the limitations of our virtues and of the wisdom of forbearance in dealing with weaker nations, can believe in the possibility of world organization responsive to the leadership and liberal ideals of the United States, then we too will have a vision which may sustain us in time of adversity and raise us above the tumbling confusion of day-to-day events. It would be a vision fit to pit against the Communist myth; a vision behind which the energies and idealism of our own and other nations could be enlisted; a vision which has more chance of fulfilment than has the Communist dream.

It is important to realize that, even after another war from which the United States emerged victorious, conflicts would not come to an end and that only a supreme international authority, with overwhelming military force at its immediate command, could settle such conflicts without fresh wars. The more vividly and carefully Americans think over these things, the more they share with other nations and peoples the task of building up such an authority—now in time of cold war as much as in a more distant future—the more satisfactory and stable will a future government of the world become. If we fail to build, little by little, an international power-wielding structure in whose counsels our allies will find a place commensurate with their strength, then we run a tremendous risk of defeat at Russia's hands; and, even should that be escaped, our descendants might find themselves forced to establish a world tyranny to protect a hard-won victory against the discontent of the other peoples of the world whose wishes and interests American policy had disregarded.

We ought to stretch our minds to such far horizons, for only so can we prepare ourselves for the high responsibility which great national power has brought and will bring. High-minded idealism has its place in any effort to prepare for the future. So far as national selfishness can be overcome, Americans will cease to regard themselves as separate from the rest of mankind and will be the better able to lead. A vivid realization of the basis of power in military force is also necessary; and, if we and our allies prove wise, a military force capable of keeping the peace of the world may emerge from the cold war itself, perhaps to be tested and tempered in a third world war, but—we can still hope—perhaps not. How broad the future base of sovereign world power can be will depend on the degree of harmony and mutual confidence which has arisen among the nations of the free world. Each day that passes offers the American people and government a chance to broaden and confirm that harmony by active co-operation with other nations in the military and economic undertakings which our security and welfare and their security and welfare alike require. The way will be long and difficult. Eventual success cannot be guaranteed. But effort may bring great results; how great cannot be told until we try.

3

The view of present and future presented in this book may seem repellent to some, unrealistic to others. I do not imagine that events will exactly follow the paths I have sketched, and I can conceive wide and drastic variations from them. Yet, in spite of all the defects in the most careful estimate of the future a man can make, it seems to me that a long view such as I have tried to take may provide a useful correction to the confusion of daily events and may even help to guide choices and frame opinions on immediate issues.

It may also have an even greater value, for by placing our own time in a large historical framework and forecasting the eventual emergence of something that seems to contain the possibility of a better and more stable world society, one may indulge in a sort of heroic optimism. I firmly believe that in future ages men will look back on the twentieth century with wonder, perhaps even with awe. They will feel—so I am convinced—that we lived in mighty and heroic times, in times when great issues hung in the balance, and when great deeds were demanded of men.

Not all ages are heroic. Sometimes a smooth current of custom and habit runs from life to life, and one generation fades into another without making any great mark on the face of the world. But our age is not such a one. Changes of vast import are under way. They seem almost sure to involve destruction and violence, as changes nearly always do. They will remake society from the pattern which has hitherto existed; and we, living in these troubled and tempestuous times, are the men whose acts will give immediate shape to the new society as it emerges. To have such a role thrust upon us is a challenge which should enlarge our minds; should make us feel we walk as giants in the earth, with the strength and opportunity, nay, the necessity, to imprint on generations yet unborn the marks of our wisdom and kindliness or lack thereof.

Such a conviction is a valuable counterweight to the mournful spirit of self-commiseration so widespread among us. There have certainly been times in which life was easier, in which decisions were less drastic and urgent; but there have seldom if ever been times when men could feel that they held the whole balance of the future in their hands as we do now. There have seldom been ages in which the full stature of a man counted for more. Wisdom, resolution, forbearance, and courage may have great results; their opposites will bring equally great disaster.

With an inner buoyancy and sense of greatness founded upon opinions such as I have put forward in this book we can face the troubles and dangers which come crowding daily to our door with a sort of high equanimity. We are living at a great moment in history. Few generations have had such responsibility and such power thrust upon them. May we not accept the challenge, take up the burden resolutely, and go forth bravely to build a peaceful and, perhaps, a better world?

INDEX

Abacus, 41

Abbasside caliphate, 42

Africa, 7, 16, 17, 27, 43, 53, 58, 59, 61, 71, 83, 93, 99, 102, 141

Agriculture, 7, 15, 16, 17, 18, 28, 32–33, 34, 36–37, 54, 56–57, 94, 177

Alaska, 140

Alchemy, 41

Alexander of Macedon, 78, 79

America; see New World; United States of America

Americanism, 121, 134, 203

Americans, 1, 55, 57, 61–62, 101, 133, 185, 186, 188–90, 193, 195, 196, 198–211

Amur River, 57

Arabs, 14, 15, 22, 39, 41, 42, 103; see also Islam

Argentina, 73, 84

Aristotle, 46

Asia, 7, 19, 20, 42, 43, 44, 45, 46, 56, 61, 71, 83, 93, 98, 99, 103, 106, 120, 127, 128, 200, 201–2

Assyria, 179

Athens, 10

Atom bomb, 135, 136

Australia, 27, 34, 51, 59, 71

Austria, 81, 130, 202

Aztecs, 52

Babylonia, 22, 179

Bacon, Francis, 47

Baltic Sea, 35

Belgian Congo, 84

Belgium, 34

Benedict of Nursia, 35

Black Sea, 35

Bolshevik Revolution, 3, 50, 56, 80, 105

Britain, 71, 77, 81, 88, 205; see also England

Buddhism, 29

Byzantium, 126, 170

Caesar, 188

Canada, 55, 133, 140

Capitalism, 89, 122, 208

Carthage, 142

Caste, 167–69

Central America, 52

China, 14, 21, 23, 24, 26, 28, 29, 34, 35, 38, 39, 41, 42, 44, 45, 56–57, 61, 63, 93, 95–96, 98, 102–4, 107, 112, 124–30, 140, 151, 166, 173–74, 179

Christianity, 29, 111, 170–71

Civil rights, 204–5

Classical civilization, 26, 35; see also Greek civilization

Cold war, 75–76, 80, 82–83, 90–92, 105–7, 119, 121, 123, 129–32, 189–90, 197–202, 204

Colonialism, 51–54, 58–59, 61, 78, 98–99

Cominform, 209

Comintern, 145

Communism, 80, 87, 105, 106, 112–13, 121, 128, 130–32, 136, 156–58, 165, 193–96, 200, 202, 203, 204–5, 206, 207–10

Communist world, 75, 76, 124, 129, 130, 141, 142, 197–201

PHOENIX BOOKS
in History

PHOENIX BOOKS
in Political Science and Law

PHOENIX BOOKS
in Philosophy and Religion

PHOENIX BOOKS
Sociology, Anthropology, and Archeology